FROM THE STREETS
TO
SCOTLAND YARD

Co-written by Louise Payne and Gwenton Sloley

FROM THE STREETS TO SCOTLAND YARD

Originally published in Great Britain by Gwenton Sloley and Louise Payne in 2010

This book is an autobiography. Places and people mentioned are true to the Authors recollection. Some people's names have been changed for confidentially reasons.

Author: Gwenton Sloley
Co-author Louise Payne
Phototypeset: Turae, Eon Graphics Ltd
Proof reading and critique: Gavin Knight
Copy editor: Harriett Wilson

ISBN: 978-1-4467-6185-4

www.fromthestreetstoscotlandyard.com

fromthestreetstoscotlandyard@yahoo.co.uk

DEDICATION

This book is dedicated to Gwendolyn Hamilton,
May you rest in peace.
And
To my son
Qwenton Sloley.
Daddy did it so you'll never have too.

ACKNOWLEDGEMENTS

First and foremost I would like to say thank you to my angel Leann, and the children. It's been a long road and you've stuck by me every step of the way. Thank you for keeping me going when I wanted to stop.

To my loyal friend and Brother Robin Travis, You've been by my side when I was in hell in prison, and stuck by my side when everyone turned against me. Your loyalty is real and I will always respect you for that.

Leann Bedeau thanks for all your great ideas and much appreciated criticism. And to everyone who believed in me Leroy Logan, Viv Ahmun, Steve,Leslie,Indran,Remi,Karen,Jada,Minara,Char,Alistair,Zoma,Amy, Alton, Ian, Hannah, Rod, Stavin, Sebastian, Andrez ,Leanne, Ibrahin, Lawrence, Jacqui, Vicky, Samson, Doc low, Funke, Rahana, PC Ed, PC Emlyn Brian, Jelise Catherine Briody, Paula Wilkinson, Jody, Rudolph ,John Rico, Paul Anstee, all of the Rush croft staff, Sterlin, Shane J, Stilts, Klint, Poky, Uncle Less, Kev and Ren Brothers.

Last but not least Mrs Valerie (Robin's Mother) you kept both me and Robin on the right track and saved us from hurting ourselves as well as others. Thank you.

CHAPTER: ONE |

As I turned over in my bed and stirred in the middle of the night, I noticed that two things weren't right. First, Uncle Clive, my father's 36-year old brother who was staying with us at the time wasn't in his bed. Second, I could hear raised voices, which I knew could only be one thing.

Mum and Dad were having another argument.

"Let she go, Carlton. You nah fi grips up de woman sah," I heard Uncle Clive say in his Jamaican accent as I drew back my bed-sheet and positioned myself upright.

I strained my eyes in the dark and watching as a dark female figure ran fearing for her life. Down the hall and out through the yard door. Twelve minutes later I was out the house, bare-footed and running down the same muddy path that lead to 4 mile close. The only other residence in Jamaica I called home.

"Ma!" I whispered, choked up by the sight before me. The two women huddled together. My mum, a woman of five feet nothing, small, slim and petite with dark brown skin and long

Indian hair that dropped into big curls at the ends sobbing in Auntie Val's arms. Auntie Val, a little over four feet tall, fair-skinned, short and round although, much smaller than my mother, comforted her with a gentle embrace and a soothing rocking motion.

"Its okay, Gwenton, go on home. Your mama's okay," Auntie Val said, acknowledging me in her home.

I loved Aunt Val. She always knew how to make us laugh no matter how bad a situation. I remember her making a joke to my mum that same night. "Gwen!" she'd said with much attitude. "You lucky you see! You should be 'appy you 'ave ah man fi fight wid' cos' mi 'ere sexy an' still corn fine one."

"I'm fine, baby. Go back before they notice you're gone," my mother said with fear in her voice.

It was dark outside. Yet when I'd left behind my mother well into the hours of the morning I had acted on instinct. My only fear at the time was of my mother's safety. Now I would have to return into the dark night alone and scared.

Without a single light to guide me I ran back up the muddy dirt path leading to our big white house and crept back in through the yard door and slipped into bed. Uncle Clive groaned in his sleep then mumbled something before filling the room with loud snores. Mum didn't come back that night nor the night after that. I think she and Dad needed the time apart, because when she did come back things were back to normal in the Sloley household.

My family consisted of my mother, Gwendolyn, whom I called Mum, my father, Carlton, and my sister, Faye, my mother's first child, ten years older than me. I was raised mostly by her: she was mum, sister, and best friend rolled in one. We all lived together in a big white house in St James Jamaica. I loved everything about our home, the long veranda that cased the house and the large steps that sat neatly at the entrance. The only thing I remember hating about our home was that it came with a monthly visitor Mr. Smith, our landlord. Mr. Smith was a man of fair skin complexion.

He looked to be in his early seventies, face as solid as a rock and continuously had his lips in a miserable pout. He never spoke: he didn't have to. We all knew what he had come for. His rent. A constant reminder that this house wasn't ours.

My father, Carlton was a smart and proud man, who set out to break the cycle of hereditary poverty and provide a new life of opportunity for his own family. He was a well-respected person amongst the locals in the area and people would often come to gather advice on how to stay strong during hard times. Ninety percent of the people on the small island that we lived on experienced poverty and struggled with the day to day hustle of life.

My parents met in 1980, and became best friends. For a year they stayed in contact over the phone as my mum was living in England and my dad was living in Jamaica, each trying to find happiness far from home. In 1981 they married and moved to Saint James, Jamaica where they settled with my sister until they had me.

On a rainy Tuesday morning in October I was their first born child and they named me Gwenton, after themselves, the first half of my mum's name and the end of my dad's. In some ways I was like my father, and in others, I was like my mother. I took personality traits from each of my parents and I resembled them both.

My round face and smooth dark-brown complexion is like my mum's and the prominent nose and brown eyes are like my Dad. Besides the cut above my right eye, I have my dad's full lips and smile, along with his physique and broad shoulders.

Although my family was deemed poor we were content until my father started gambling heavily. The constant loss of our finances caused arguments with my mum, so there was always a lot of drama in our house. Mum, who devoted her life to the church in some ways understood what Dad was going through and she really felt for the man she married. She knew he really loved his family and he wanted to be a good provider, but when he found it difficult to keep his money it really stressed him out.

Dad's brother, Uncle Clive stayed with us for six weeks before he showed strong signs of withdrawal symptoms from the city. Both he and Dad were raised in Saint Elizabeth then moved to Montego Bay in the late 1970s. Uncle Clive was a short, stocky man with dark-brown skin and short black hair like both me and my father. He was a loving, peaceful man that got along with everyone, but at the same time liked his own company. Uncle Clive didn't socialize much when he came to stay and he would always dress in his own mix-matched threads and used out of town lingo to match. Although he was a hard worker, he never seemed to be able to make money. My father, on the other hand, was quite the opposite, quite capable of making money and soon made plans to leave Jamaica to look for a better source of income, leaving both me and my mother behind.

Faye showed no objections towards my father leaving. Although they had their differences, I loved him very much, but I hated the gambling and fights.

Dad always used to say to me "Watch da space around you, son, and time will tell!"

Being young I paid no attention to what he'd said. In my mind I imagined my father returning a rich man. I had no objections with his departure despite the fact that with him gone my mother became the disciplinarian of the household. She knew how to put down a beating.

If she told you to do something and you didn't do it she would yell "Gwenton, mi not going to talk again," and then she would beat the shit out of you for the mere fact of having to repeat herself. I remember this one day it had been raining the whole morning so Faye and I had to stay inside. By late after-noon we were dying of boredom and decided to play in the rain, we raced up and down the tiled veranda laughing and splashing until I slipped and smacked my face on the floor.

"Gwenton!!" Faye screamed, rushing over and scooping me off the ground as I wailed. By now our mum was making her way towards the house. The first thing she saw was the pool of blood where we stood, and then my hysterical reaction to the new scar I'd sport for the rest of my life above my right eye. It really wasn't as bad as it seemed but because the blood started mixing with the rain water the dark fluid extended extensively.

"Ah, wah mi tell you?" she said with one hand on her hip and pointing her finger, she putting all the blame on Faye.

"How old are you?" she repeated while she whooped her any which way she could. It hurt to see Faye take the blame like that because we were only playing, but she was a trooper. Her beating lasted a whole five minutes in counting and that was a long time when it was time to get yours.

During the first few years of my childhood my mother and father made many trips out of town to America then to England where my father later settled. He made constant attempts to remedy the situation at home, sending money, small items of clothing, but it wasn't enough. Mum would joke about his new life out there. Making up stories, she'd say, "Gwent, trust mi know your dad gon ova dere and ah woman sweet im up an dat's why im don't want fi come back." Yet her child like jokes soon became reality.

I guess after so many fights, even two people who love each other can grow apart.

When dad left for England in 1990, I saw my mother change. Though sad she didn't cry at his departure she hardened up, and simply carried on as if nothing had changed. A woman of five feet nothing, but the bravest woman I've ever known. I loved her dearly. Growing up I'd seen and heard things that nowadays would be considered a domestic dispute, my mother screaming out for help or my father punching a wall. In my eyes my mother was as hard as nails, I looked up to her. She made me feel safe.

I watched her swallow her pride in order for us to survive, constantly forced to work degrading jobs just so we could eat. I was a growing boy, and even at the age of six I had started wanting

13

things I'd see other children have at school. I had now become one of the children that didn't know their dad. When asked where my dad was, I found my opportunity to make up such stories like: He's in the army or he's a policeman! I told these lies so I wouldn't get picked on as I knew my dad would never be coming to pick me up from school again.

For two Christmas's in a row I got a water gun, the same make and style just in a different colour because my mum had no money to buy me anything more. Often I thought about my mother having to wash other people's clothes to make ends meet. Now I felt hatred towards some of her friends because I thought of them as family. I would call them "Auntie," yet they had no objections towards my mother hand washing their dirty linen.

My mother did what she had to do being that the situation was particularly critical in our developing country especially since we lived where the majority of the poor lived. Not everyone in Jamaica was poor though, many had family living in England or the State's who were financially able to send support while others were born into a family who owned large amounts of land enabling them to grow crops and raise livestock that would thrive for generations. Nor my father or mother were amongst those people, we were alone on the island even more so when my father left. Living in poverty faced lasting obstacles that kept our fellow Jamaican's from attaining their most basic human rights and individual potentials. Lacking adequate food, shelter, access to education and healthcare, protection from violence, and a voice in what happens in their communities. They live day to day and in constant fear of the future. My mother had seen firsthand how poverty depletes families' economic, physical, and psychological resources, drains their coping abilities, and exhausts their social support networks. In short, it inhibits families' and communities' ability to care for themselves and their children. Many people fell into the stereotype "Yardie" due to their perceived lower financial status. In the following years, gang violence or behaviour on the part of Jamaicans became known in wider British society as "Yardie

14

culture" and the participants "Yardie's". The terms "Yardie gang" or "Yardie gun violence" were largely used by the British media to described violent crimes in the black community. Men and women would sometimes risk their lives to cross over into the British seas either by smuggling drugs or seeking illegal asylum.

My father's departure was a major turning point in my life. I was both curious and impressionable, deeply in need of a strong father figure in my life.

With Mum consumed with work I subconsciously searched for a male to step in and guide me like a father would do. Little did I know I wouldn't have to wait long before my dad and I were reunited. Two years later, I was eight and my dad had sent me a ticket to join him in England.

CHAPTER: TWO |

Squinting from the rays of the bright scorching sun, I paced myself as I reached level ground. I'd long given up riding my bicycle and had begun pushing it down this huge hill that ventured from the top of my house to the back yard when I felt the urge to *simply smile*.

Beaming with happiness, I reached the veranda where my mother stood, hand on hip, waiting.

I was going to England to spend the six week holiday with my father and the rest of his family of whom only a few relatives I had met. I was excited, in fact, I was ecstatic. I remember waving good bye to my mother with the biggest smile on my face, but as I boarded the plane a sense of guilt confronted me. Cold and alone, I was abandoning her.

The seven hour flight from Montego Bay, Jamaica to London Gatwick airport left me feeling nauseous and uneasy. Situated at the very front of the plane and accompanied by five other children, in whom two were in the custody of an air-hostess, I cried most of the journey already missing home. Once on the ground, I wiped my eyes with the back of my hand and followed my guardian as other passengers departed the plane. The children who I was accompanied by had long departed the plane in Canada en route to the United States.

Surrounded by people of all colours rushing around in different directions bumping and shoving one another I was taken aback by my surroundings. My guardian located my baggage shortly after our departure of the plane and we waited. I stood holding the tall blond woman's hand in the middle of the large white and glass building. The sweet smell of the cold air conditioning confirmed I had made my destination. Finally I spotted a familiar face. Two.

My attention at the time was devoted to a smartly dressed white family of four as they greeted one another with long hugs. This one lady, while squatting, held her arms wide open for a little red dress-wearing pig-tailed girl to venture into.

I fought back tears when Aunt Bobs and Grandma approached me.

"You not gonna give ya auntie a hug, Gwenton?" She said stretching out her arms like the lady I'd seen before them had done. Aunt Bobs tried to get me to warm to her and though coy, I walked into her tight embrace and found myself hugging her back. It had been a long time since I'd seen my family in England, but I could never forget Aunt Bobs or Grandma.

Grandma, my father's mother, resembled the late actress Marilyn Monroe, her jet black hair always seemed to shimmer like silk. I'd often heard people back home refer to her type of hair as coolly. Grandma was short and stocky and in her late fifties but very youthful. She had a kind heart and a calm persona. Still she was not one to tolerate crap from anyone. Aunt Bobs, one of the middle children and was the image of her mother accept younger.

"You remember ya Aunt Bobs, don't you?"

"Yes." Nodding,) I released from her embrace and went into the greeting arms of my Grandma. She smelled the same way she did in 1989 when I'd last visited England, warm and secure like a mother would.

"Look how he grown? He favours Carlton bad."

"You big now, Gwenton!" I listened to Grandma and Aunt Bobs compliment me on how I'd grown and how much I looked like my father before we began to make our way to the entrance of the airport.

"Where's my dad?" I asked as we walked quickly through the thick crowd of holiday goers huddled by the extremely large automatic doors.

"He's at the house, sugar!" Grandma warmly smiled, letting me know we were heading to her house. I couldn't wait to see my dad. Outside was cold compared to the stifling heat in Jamaica, but being that it was late June my attire did not feel inappropriate. The walk to the train station was quiet as was the train ride home, mainly because although lovely people, both Grandma and Aunt Bobs were quiet and tamed. Besides the odd "You all right" and "You okay" we pretty much travelled in silence.

***

Like Grandma had said back at the airport my father was back at her house awaiting my arrival. We had eaten a typical Caribbean style dinner of rice and peas, stewed-Chicken, macaroni and cheese and steamed vegetables then said our good-byes, promising to visit on the following weekend. I waved good-bye to my grandma from the taxi window then turned to my father and smiled.

I was staring at my dad while he was engaged in idle chit chat with the driver, but I didn't care, I was just happy to finally have him to myself. We drove through Bruce Grove in Tottenham. I'd only been to England once before, but I would never forget the day Aunt Bobs brought me around that area to a toy store where she bought me some of my most prized possessions as a child. For a majority of the drive, my thought's drifted back to Jamaica. And I remembered how I'd cried on the plane as my mum waved me off. I hated leaving her behind.

But, I was only going to be here for six weeks. I didn't want to think about my life back in Jamaica while I was in England, but I couldn't help it. I thought of an evening when me and my mum were walking to the bus stop: it was about nine at night. I remember it was late because it was a week night and I had to meet her after school. I'd met her at her place of work where she looked after a little girl from a wealthy family who lived quite a distance from us. I hoped that with one less mouth to feed for six weeks my mother wouldn't have to subject herself to such labour.

The driver pulled the taxi to a halt. I glanced out the window and was amazed by the large steel silver gates opposite us that led to the entrance of an underground car park.

"Right here, tank you," my dad spoke to the driver. I'd lost count of how many times I'd smiled that day. *He talked to the English people with his Jamaican accent,* I thought to myself, happy that England hadn't changed him.

Both the driver and my father continued to exchange words through the small glass window that separated the driver from the passengers. I shared no interest in what they were saying. I was taken aback by the building before me. My angelic mind looked up and out of my passenger side window, saw the steel gates and believed my father owned the whole estate.

I can't believe my father owns all this and he's just come to England. I'd always known that England was a wealthy country because of my mum's child like jokes.

"Your dad's ova dere rich and don't wah send us more than some lickle joke change," I heard her saying in my head as I hoped out the taxi. I giggled.

"You ahright, Gwent?" he asked beaming with pride. My dad playfully put his hand on my head and exhaled.

"Yes, daddy," I replied, unable to hide the bright smile we both shared. I handed him my suitcase and followed as he led the way up a flight of stairs and led to a long balcony where he stopped at the last brown door on the right.

I waited in anticipation as he searched his pockets for the key; I couldn't wait to see what his home looked like from the inside.

I held my breath when instantly hit with a strong scent the moment my dad opened the front door. I was familiar with the smells of certain traditional burning incense because we often used them, but still, as I entered my father's mini-mansion I couldn't help but think of the Rastafarians whose houses held this smell back home in Jamaica.

"Come. Dis way." Dad said. He rested my luggage by the entrance of the sitting room door, gesturing with his hand for me to go on inside. I walked slowly to his side where I stood in front of the two other occupants of his home.

"Dis here is you Auntie Joyce and her son Klinton!" he explained before briefly leaving the room. There was a moment of awkward silence between the three of us, two who had remained seated. I looked at my new Auntie Joyce and cousin Klinton and tried to think of who in my family they resembled. Joyce was a tad bit lighter than the people in my family as was her son; she wore her hair in tight curls and wore plenty gold chains and rings.

"You want a drink, darling? An ice pole, maybe?" These were amongst some of the things Auntie Joyce offered me, attempting to break the ice.

"No tank you," I'd nod my head and reply each time. I wasn't accustomed to taking things from strangers, even if this lady was my auntie. We had never met; already I was beginning to feel uncomfortable in her presence and was glad when my father returned.

"Klint, why don't you take Gwenton upstairs to play?" Aunt Joyce spoke again.

I stood dumb founded looking at my dad; I didn't know what

to do.

"Go 'head. Leave your bags dere, sah and go." Again I smiled at how much he had remained the same then hurried behind Klinton, who was already half way up the tall flight of stairs on the left hand side of the hall.

I burned with envy the moment Klinton swung his bedroom door open and flopped down onto the bed. The room was painted in dark blue with two large windows over-looking the garden. Pictures of cartoon characters covered the walls with drawing pins. He had a double bed and a large wooden table on which he had stacked all his computer games. Next to his computer was the small black and white TV. On the far side of the room was a small two door black wardrobe. It was nothing like I'd ever seen.

Klinton two years older than me, brown-skinned with two big rabbit like upper teeth,) would be eleven after the summer and would be starting a secondary school. His exterior came across as a shy mummy's boy but he would later come out of his shell.

At that moment in time I knew Klinton didn't care for me, but that was fine by me: I was only going to be there for the summer then I was going back home. Slowly, I walked into Klinton's bedroom and watched as he sprang into action plugging in his SNES (Super Nintendo Entertainment System). Taking a seat at the edge of his bed, I marvelled over all the possessions in his room. I ran my eyes over shelves, bookcases, and the top of the wardrobe and even peeked under the bed. To say Klinton was privileged was an understatement. He may not have been your ordinary white collar boy, but struggle hadn't called his name.

***

"I'm tired, Daddy!"

After two hours I had climbed down the stairs rubbing my eyes and was tugging on my father's shirt. It had been a long day and I was ready to collapse into a thick British duvet like the ones Klinton had on his bed.

"Go on back upstairs, I soon come!" he said. Relaxed, my dad returned his attention back to the television set that sat in the far right corner of the room. On the opposing wall was a long glass cabinet filled with ornaments and China plates that as long as I'd lived in that house were never used. I think Aunt Joyce was saving them for the day the queen popped in. At first glance, I'd assumed there were at least four bedrooms as I had counted a number of doors coming off the upstairs hallway. Like my dad instructed, I returned to Klinton's room and sat on the end of his bed watching as he controlled Super Mario on his high-tec computer system. Something I could have only dreamed of owning in Jamaica. Occasionally he too glanced up at me, but neither of us spoke.

My ears perked up at the sound of my dad and Aunt Joyce making their way up the stairs. I heard them switching off the down stairs lights then watched as my dad walked past Klinton's bedroom, disappearing behind a door at the far end of the hallway. Aunt Joyce pulled clean sheets out of a cupboard that I'd earlier presumed was a room.

"Come on, Klint, turn that computer off and yous lot get ready for bed." She handed us the clean sheets. To my understanding *"Yous"* meant *"You lot,"* *the both of you.* Naturally, I helped Klinton change his bedding. I thought *after we changed his were gonna do mine.* Yet it had not gone un-noticed that there was only one bed in Klinton's room. I spent many years in Jamaica sharing a bed with my sister. I was accustomed to sharing many things in Jamaica, but this was different. Klinton was a stranger and I *knew* he didn't like me. For the first time since my arrival I wanted to be back home.

With the clean bedding now on the bed. I positioned myself right back on the edge and watched Klinton carefully wrap the wires up for his control pads and placed them neatly beside the system. The sound of a door opening caused me to look towards the hallway.

Something ain't right here. I told myself as my I watched my dad emerge from his bedroom in nothing but a pair of Y-Fronts and a T-Shirt. I turned over and looked at Klinton. I could hear my dad using the toilet then watched dumb founded as he said goodnight then returned to his room.

"Goodnight," Aunt Joyce said standing in the doorway and smiling before retiring to the very same room I'd seen my dad disappear into. I looked at Klinton again; he was settled under his duvet pressed up against the wall. It was then it hit me. *This woman wasn't my aunt, we are no relation.* Pulling back the duvet on what was now established as my side of the bed I got in and lay stiff next to Klinton, pretend to be asleep, except with my eyes wide opened.

There must be another room in there. I desperately tried to come up with an alternative reason why my dad would not only feel comfortable walking around his sister's home half naked, but also share a room with her. But deep down I knew what it was and I hated it. I closed my eyes as my mother's words filled my thoughts. *"You daddy fine ah woman ova dere wah sweet em dat's why em no come back."*

CHAPTER: THREE |

Spending my summer holiday on Stoke Newington Estate was far from the holiday I'd hoped for. For one it had been made very obvious that Aunt Joyce was not my auntie but in fact my step-mother to be and at every opportunity Klinton made it clear that he detested me being in his room.

"I just don't like him touching my things," he'd whine when he thought I wasn't around. I once heard him ask his mum when I'd be going home.

"It won't be long, son!" I heard her say. That was the first time I ever felt unwanted. I wanted to scream, "I've got my own house with my own bed! I don't even want to be here!" But what could I do, I was just a child. Eventually, as my six week holiday ended and having not returned to Jamaica, I learned to deal with my isolated feelings and ventured out onto the estate.

Like yesterday I can remember walking with my hands deep in my pockets, dragging my feet through the small brown patches of grass that posed as a communal playing ground for the hundred and some residents of Victoria Grove. I thought *this is it. I'm finally going to put Landry on his back.* Landry made me sick walking around the estate like he owned the place, always telling us younger boys to get out the football pitch and jacking (Robbing) us for our change.

It was the middle of July 1993, the beginning of a long summer holiday. Still, I was consumed with complications at home.

From the shared balcony of the small flat I had been made to call home I'd watched Landry, one of the youngest local bullies pick on some of the smaller kids on the block before I decided I wanted him defeated.

It was cold outside, yet the sharp English weather biting my skin was the least important thing on my mind, Earlier that afternoon I had allowed myself to be a child again, watching cartoons.

Michael Angelo, Leonardo, Donatello, Rafael. Those animated *Ninja Turtles* had nothing on the type of moves the kids around the estate would pull on you if you didn't watch your back.

Structured to be a secure residential area with shared communal grounds and parking, Stoke Newington through my eyes reminded me more of an elderly residential site than a gang-infused community.

The strong smell of piss stung my nose as I walked past a stairwell of one of the fifteen identical Massenet styled buildings that surrounded me making up the whole of Victoria Grove Estate.

With my small hands balled into fists still buried deep in my pockets, I had allowed my eight-year old mind to convince myself that if I continued to study some of the moves on the Ninja Turtles, it wouldn't be long before I'd learn to defend myself amongst the small gangs made up of local bullies that occupied the communal grounds daily.

"Yo' Que!"

I watched from the corner of my eye as Landry cupped his hands around his mouth and shouted, trying to get my attention when he spotted me walking across the foot path that connected all the dirt brown buildings together. Since coming to England everybody now called me Que, Gwenton seemed to hard for the English tongue they had a habit of pronouncing the "G" as a "Q" even family members started calling me Que. I liked it though Gwenton felt like the poor me and I was in England now, Que sounded rich, successful and English.

"Oi!"

Still I ignored him yet continued in his direction.

"You don't hear me talking to you!"

He raised the tempo of his voice, eager to show me who was boss.

Just minutes away from where Landry stood scoping the grounds for prey I prepared myself for the worst. I was nervous, but I wasn't scared. Weeks ago when I'd first met Landry he'd told me he was nine, a year older than I was at the time, but he looked more like twelve. In fact he was twice my size with strong African features that made him resemble a man far beyond his years. Largely built with skin so dark it was almost a shade of blue, he was strong. I knew this first hand the last time we'd fought he'd got in a lucky blow.

Within the first two minutes he'd sucker punched me so hard in my stomach that he'd knocked the wind out of me. Something told me this time would be different.

"You gonna hit me back this time?" he asked shoving me as hard as he could while he spoke. Landry found satisfaction in watching me stumble.

I kept telling myself, *do it like the ninja turtles,* as I tussled with him and it was working until Landry hit me with a blow to the gut that took me off my feet. I doubled over in pain; Landry was whooping my ass. I was no match for him and he knew it. I froze, steady trying to think of a route of escape. It was then I noticed someone was watching. Klinton. My step brother. We caught each other's eye and he read my mind. It was on.

"Get off my brother, you punk!"

Klinton yelled as he grabbed Landry by the shoulders and threw him off me. Even then I was quick on my feet and was up before Landry had hit the ground.

We beat the hell out of him that day and laughed about it later while we hung out in the room we shared. That day was the closest me and Klinton had been since I'd moved into the house my father shared with him and his mother, but it was a prime example of how bonds were formed in the streets.

I would never go as far as to say that bridges were built at home, but I can admit that with me and Klinton joining forces the atmosphere there was more accommodating. Though I didn't have any more disputes with Klinton my step-mother continued to make my life difficult. First, by disconnecting the current phone number so my mother and I couldn't verbally keep in contact (I would now only be in contact with her through letters), Then amongst other things on occasion, when she and my father would have arguments which usually ended in him going up-stairs to his room and only coming out to use the toilet, for revenge she'd refuse to cook. Instead, she'd order take out for herself and Klinton. That's how I learnt how to cook. I would make corned-beef and rice or sometimes with dumplings. It was always the same with my step-mother. I don't think she ever considered me a part of her family, yet I was forced to consider her a part of mine.

Soon the summer of 1995 rapidly approached and I was due to start secondary school the following term. England had now become my home.

I dreaded the idea of starting a school filled with rowdy English youth like the ones that lived on my estate, but I anticipated my return to Jamaica before the start of term. It would be the first time I'd see my mother since I'd left for England in 1992, and unbeknownst to me it would also be the last time I would see her in good health.

I was ecstatic to be back in Jamaica, around the only family I'd ever known. Using my accent again came natural and it felt great. I'd never forget the day my mum sent me to the corner shop to buy salt. She was cooking rice and needed it to take away the starchy freshness.

"Can I get a bag of salt please?" I asked the tall man behind the counter who had really paid me no mind.

"Ah wah?" he turned to me and asked. Now that I had his full attention.

"Salt," I repeated.

"Ah wah 'im say, Rudi?" the shop owner asked his friend who also couldn't understand what I was saying.

"Sarlt," I finally said after the sixth time of pronouncing the word.

"Ohhh, Sarlt. Why you neva say so." Reaching behind him, the friend handed me a bag of salt while the shop owner counted my dollars. Even when I used my best Jamaican accent they still said I sounded like a country boy.

I loved spending time with my mum. Her eyes filled with love each and every time she looked my way. She beamed with pride when people complimented her on how well I'd grown. I was happy. Happier than I'd been in a long time. I didn't once feel like I was in the way like I did in England. Here I was complete. Despite the differences in the two lifestyles, I despised the thought of returning to England. In my mind, there would be no other place I'd call home except Jamaica.

I begged my mum "Please Mum, let me stay I don't want to go back there it's not what you thinks I hate it. Please Mum," I stressed on the way to the airport, but my pleas fell on deaf ears.

"Gwenton, don't worry bout me. I will be fine I'm a fighter, but dere is nothing but war here an dis isn't for you, baby." She looking into my eyes and told me moment before I was due to board the plane.

Loving my mother dearly made it easy for me to heed her advice. I was almost knocking on eleven, a minor still but even then I knew she wouldn't steer me wrong. I'd seen it with my own eyes how almost every Jamaican I'd known or even met had some type of fixation of making it to "foreign" as they referred to the United

Kingdom.

Many made it their main objective in life, while some put the thought before education and their own welfare. Others put the thought of a better life before their freedom and would smuggle drugs for the top man in the area in return for a ticket.

Before boarding the plane, I hugged my mother tight and reassured her of my good behaviour while I'm away. This time as we departed I didn't cry for as the plane took off I was sure I'd be coming back. But I was mistaken.

When I returned to England the letters from my mother stopped. With a week to go before I was to start secondary school I was desperate for her. The pain of not being able to hear her voice was unbearable. It killed me that Klinton's father was allowed to call the house when he wanted without the same type of hostility. It wasn't until I got older that I understood the reason behind my step-mothers actions. Although she pretended to care about me, all of her caring was to make my dad happy. But once there was an argument she would make it clear that it was her money we were all living off.

She would say, "Your dad didn't bring any money home this week. You know why? Because he bet it all on the horses so you should be grateful." She could be the nicest person you could meet, as long as you did what she wanted, and when you didn't, often there were severe consequences.

Deliberately trying to commit suicide when I was around, my step-mother made sure she was the victim in all her and my father's major disputes. She remained insecure where my father and mother were concerned. They hadn't yet divorced and remained Mr. and Mrs. Sloley. I guess having your lover's wife calling was too much for my step-mum to handle.

I must have been about eleven at the time and I remember this one evening my dad sent me to the shop to buy a loaf of bread. By now I was used to the roughness of the estate and was well known around the blocks. I decided to take the long way around and went to the shop on the high road because I wanted to play outside for another ten minutes. Plus I'd met up with my close friend, Roderick who resembled the singer Lloyd, even down to his coolly hair, except he was a lot darker. Roderick got all the girls our age on the estate. We joked about as we walked back to my house. Roderick had to pass my house before he got to his own block and we both had to be in at the same time on week days, 7:30pm. So we would ask at home what was needed at the shops knowing there was always something our parents wanted but would not go get it themselves.

"What time you passing mines in the morning?" Roderick asked me, we'd continued our chatter towards my block.

"Bout eight and don't be late." I told Roderick as he held out his fist for a pound. I was about to show him love before we departed (Our way of saying goodbye), but was distracted by the smoke coming from one of the underground garage's where my step-mum used to park her car.

"No woman, no cry, No woman, no cry." Bob Marley's classic blared from the scene.

I looked at Roderick and he looked at me. We both knew she was trying to kill herself again, I got used to her suicide attempts; it became normal to me. The atmosphere in the house was too much for her. Eventually, she allowed her insecurities to get the better of her finally, stopping all contact from my mum. It was this type of neglect and discomfort in my surroundings that opened my heart to the streets. I had hardened as I grew mentally stronger and now had a temper that awaited its release. Inside I was cold without my mother to guide me, I was incomplete. Taken away from the very person who loved me the most and placed into a battlefield filled with mental wars. My heart had cracked, no longer that loving child with the bright smile that had come from Jamaica those five and some years ago. I was ready to accept any type of guidance offered by the local rude boys, as the rewards would be great. I started Homerton Boys School in Hackney on the 9th of September 1995. There I found the encouragement and loyalty from a family I craved for at home.

From The Streets To Scotland Yard, Gwenton Sloley

CHAPTER: FOUR |

"This way, boys!" Mr. Jones, a tall V neck woolly jumper wearing man with short dark hair shouted over the school boys' banter. Proudly leading his New Year seven form class through the main hall, intent on keeping a single file line amongst the group. It was like coming to England all over again. My Step-mother had taken the initiative of pre-booking a cab for my first day of school. And once we arrived she dropped me off at the school gate and watched as I made my way to the entrance alone. I was scared; I didn't know anyone and images of me being bullied consistently clouded my mind. I was sweating, and then again so was Mr. Jones, It must be the heat in here, and I tried to convince myself fidgeting in my uniform. As I studied my surroundings, the menacing looks I received from the other boys some who looked like men (,) their average height being five feet, I knew fear had settled in. Those glares distributed by the older boys were the gloves of intimidation and they fit snug. I knew it wouldn't be long before I'd have to defend myself again like I had done with Landry in the past. This time I was ready; I'd had plenty fights at home with Klinton. No English bwoy is gonna hold me down I almost snickered to myself then I remembered what my dad had said when I left the house that morning.

"Gwenton, no trouble ya here mi, ah ya first dey ah school." I wanted to be obedient and tried my best to put all hostility out my mind but my uncertainty was just too strong.

"Move out da way?" An older boy shoved passed me.

"Look at these lil 'nigga's" Followed by laughter I watched as some of the older boys taunted the new starters.

"Ahh!" I jumped into reflex mode.

"It's okay, you looked lost honey bee!" I'd turned back towards the entrance, being bumped left and right and tumbled into the presence of my head of year. "All the year sevens are gathering in the main hall. Come with me!" she calmly explained, placing her guiding hand on my shoulder. *How did she know I was a first year? I wondered Maybe it's because I'm shorter than most of the other boys or does she know I ain't English?* I thought as I allowed her to guide me into the wall where the other New Year sevens stood awaiting orders.

Inside the main hall I was elated to find that I wasn't alone after all. I knew a few faces from around the ends, some more than others. We'd nod, say, "What's up" or simply kept it moving. This is going to be fun, I began to assume noticing all the familiar faces where the typical "Rude bwoy's" from different locations in the ends (Hackney).

"Wah, Gwan, Que?" I heard my name as I sat down; Dean 'Greek-Stuff' Davis (as he was known on the streets) threw himself in the seat next to me and held his fist out for a pound.

"What's good, Greeks," I said as our fists touched. We sat in silence until another boy approached us. I watched them greet each other with a solid embrace before introductions were made.

"This Smithy. He my cousin!" Greeks explained returning to his seat.

"What's up Que?" Reluctantly, Smithy held out his fist and to both our surprise I showed him love. Most people who knew me at this time knew I was a lone ranger. Sure I had made some friends during my time spent in England, but I wasn't the begging friend type. If I knew you it was all good but if I didn't my guard was up. But today was different. I was in no situation to be turning friends down. Besides I liked Greeks and Smithy seemed pretty cool. Both Greeks and Smithy where of Jewish decent, yet neither of them looked like your typical Jewish school boy. For one, they didn't wear those little netted hats on their heads. Instead they sported a short back and sides cut like most boys on the roads, and were fair skinned, slightly tanned with sharp square faces. We became friends from that very first meeting and would become partners in crime in the years to follow.

Four months into the new term I'd committed my first offence. It was the first crime I'd ever committed and although I didn't get caught, I knew it was wrong. Yet there was a sense of satisfaction in my actions.

"Gwenton, would you like to collect the register and meal tickets from the main office" Mrs. Branes had asked one morning as I sat in my form class paying less attention than normal.

"Yes Miss!" I sprang to my feet, thinking of the responsibility and was glad she'd picked me out of the other 36 pupils who had their arms stretched up high hoping she'd choose them. Yet, as I returned from the main office with the register and meal tickets in hand I couldn't help but listen to the two voices in my mind.

"It's only a meal ticket Que. Rip one off. Go on, no one would know".

Don't do it Que you gonna get in trouble! Confused I thought of the repercussions, consequences and then profit. I could sell whatever I take, I thought. Each meal ticket provided its owner to any lunch of their choice including dessert. Naturally the thought of making a sale put all doubt out my mind and I found myself ripping two meal tickets off the red roll and stuffing them in my pocket. I later found out by an older boy who also collected the register for his form class that the trick was to not be greedy.

"They always be putting nine extra tickets on the roll so you can't take no more than five a day, you get me!" he'd told me once we were out of ears reach. I decided then that out of my five I'd take one and sell the rest for a pound each. By the end of the month I had twenty pounds in change in my pocket, which was more than I could say for the other boys in my year. I was loving the feeling of getting easy money. I ate like a king at lunch time and as the term slowly came to an end I had a small reputation going for myself on the playing grounds too. Fighting had become a way to earn stripes and I'd long earned myself enough to get me through the next four years of Homerton Boys 'School. With my fast reflexes and rare aggression, I'd ranked into the top five best fighters. Becoming so well known in and outside of the school gates, my school life became easy and I hardly ever had to fight, except to prove a point. Homerton Boys' school was the only school in the area ending their school day at three o'clock, giving us the advantage to get to other schools before their students were released. And when they released us, they released us. We were reckless; carrying guns to school, knives, anything that could be used as a weapon.

I was twelve the first time I saw a real gun. Jamie Dundun; a short ginger boy with freckles whose family were travellers discreetly opened his bag at morning break and showed me what his father had been hiding underneath their kitchen floor.

"It's no big deal," Jamie said as he passed me the bag for a better look "My uncle brought it over from Ireland."

"Yeah?" I said running my fingers over the steel.

"Yeah! Like I said it ain't a big deal, my uncle can get his hands on all kinds' tools. It's easy as long as you got the money for em," he told me taking the bag and closing it before he placed it on his back. Jamie was a year older than me but that didn't stop us from being friends; we would bunk off school to hang out with the older guys on the Pembury Estate. We both had people that side of the end. We must have driven the local police crazy because they

36

were continuously chasing us around the borough but we were too smart for them. We used the blocks as hideouts or sometimes we kicked it at a friend's house. There was always someone whose parents were working a 9 to 5 leaving their home vacant for us to occupy during school hours. Lucky for me the teachers never seemed to notice I was missing, I always snuck back into the school at the end of the day to sign in and made sure I was marked in during registration.

"Here Pull this?" Jamie stretched out his lanky arm and passed me half smoked cigarette. I put the bud to my lips and took a long drag filling both my lungs with smoke which caused me to break out in a coughing fit.

"Rubbish!" Jamie laughed. Taking his cigarette back he put it to his mouth and drew in the smoke "You not supposed to swallow the smoke, your meant you bring it to the back of your throat like this." He demonstrated again. That was the first and last time I tried to smoke, I just didn't see the big deal in smoking but Jamie and his two older brothers Patrick and Jack seemed to find it fun. They would stand outside the shops begging the older boys who would never decline to buy them cigarettes. Jamie and his older brothers were respected around most parts they had a big mobile family with a violent Irish background. We would sneak into Cardinal Pole a mixed school five minutes down the road from our own; our uniform was the same colour so their teachers could never tell us apart from their own students. We would chat up the girl's who loved being around us. The Cardinal Pole Boys didn't stand a chance against us Homerton Boys, are reputation had them intimidated on their own grounds. Even the teachers stood back when our fights broke out.

"Ahhhhh haaa," the crowd would laugh out when one of our smaller guys stole a punch towards one of the much bigger boys that attended a school a bus ride away from ours. Myself, Smithy, and Greeks would now sit on the wall with some of the older guys, who like me, were never required to fight. Their presence brought over the girls, which always seemed to work to my advantage.

We would all hype up each and every time we kicked it with the Olders. Being at the only boys school in your borough naturally made you a target for the opposite sex, but I was more interested in jacking (Robbing) their phones than getting any numbers. Robbing them school girls was easy too, because I always thought with my bigger head, making stealing my only objective.

Smithy and Greek's never brought me around girls they were digging. In fact none of the guys I rolled with did. Most of the Olders we hung with were from Holly Street and so was Smithy, Greeks was from Stoke Newington like me. It became a routine for us to just cotch (chill out) after school hours usually hanging around the neighbourhood in large groups making loud disturbances and being kicked out of establishments, we soon ran out of places to reside.

"You guys can't tell anyone bout this place, man found it on the weekend. I see a couple emptying it and I watched them leave out." Smithy rubbed his hands together as he prepared to show me and Greeks a place we would later spend a wide amount of our spare time. You had to bend your head a little depending how tall you were but other than that when Smithy pulled back the sheet used for coverage the space he showed us was decent. Underneath one of the tower blocks was an empty garage the same size as a two bedroom flat. Old sofa's and any miscellaneous chairs we found made it into "Cotch." That's what we called it. Pitch black once the door was close we had have to flash our phone lights to see each other. Cotch became our under world headquarters, we would plan robberies sleep with girls without been disturbed. A lot of the females in the area lost their virginity in there while the rest of us watched and on many occasions joined in.

I already had a name around Hackney. Everyone in my age group knew I wasn't the man to be messed with when it came to people's personal belongings. I started my street robberies snatching the phones of the girls that came to cotch, most of the time they didn't watch for their bags when they were on their back, and then when I got a little braver I started snatching women's handbags. I would target rich women coming from the city, get up close to them while their arm was relaxed, then yank the strap of their bag and run like hell. Not stopping until I reached the block. I owned that hustle; I was one of the fastest runners around my way so they had no chance of catching me. At times, I couldn't help but laugh when I'd see the women trying to run after me as if they really had a chance at matching my speed. One time I looked behind me and caught a chubby middle aged woman trying to give chase and I laughed so hard I caught a stitch. I slowed down to catch my breath. As she got close I took off again, only I dropped the bag still consumed with laughter. I was pissed though once I'd reached the block empty-handed and breathless, but with adrenaline still rushing through my body I felt powerful. People were starting to take me seriously and I couldn't wait to leave school to become a real gangster like some of my brother's friends, who by now would often let me hang out with them after school.

CHAPTER: FIVE |

"**Q**ue right?" Panting and still very defensive I eyed the hand on my shoulder before acknowledging the face.

"Oh, what's up?" I asked trying to remain calm and cool.

It was one of those afternoons when the sun was shining, a prime ingredient for drama in the hood. Me, Smithy, Greeks and some other youth from the area had taken to the streets as soon as school let out. No sooner had we turned the corner, all hell broke loose. While we walked a few yards from the school goofing off and girl-talking, this nuts boy named Rors came out from nowhere and started talking crazy to Greeks then our crew. He walked up trying to call us out just as my boy, Dean, and his girl walked by. So I nodded to acknowledge his presence. When I turned around, I was unaware that Greeks and Rors was about to throw down until he got in my face acting all ignorant.

"What the fuck you lil niggas gonna do, huh?" Rors asked,

acting like he wanted some from me.

"What you wanna do?" I snapped back, squaring him off with much bass in my voice. I wasn't one to get into lip service. That made a person vulnerable. When he tried to reply I socked him square in his grill so hard that spit squirted out of his mouth on contact. There we were locked up, and rolling around on the ground. I was punching him, and he was socking me back. As the fight escalated, people immediately started closing in on us to watch. I won't lie, he did get a few good licks off me, but I was tagging his ass. Of course, his boys couldn't take the pressure of me beating their boy down, so they jumped in. But once my boys got involved it was over. Suddenly, I could hear sirens. I scanned the area for my boys and could just about make out their backs as they made off, that's when I felt a hand on my shoulder.

"Let me holler at you for a minute."Coolly Lee removed his hand from where he'd rested it and motioned for me to follow him. Lee was half black and half Indian, hence the name "Coolly Lee." He was one of Klinton's associates, yet I looked up to him and wanted badly to be like him. He always had the nice clothes, the trainers, jewels and the girls loved him. He was about four feet nine, small, but well-respected in the drug industry.

"I like you, Que. you got this gangster look about you," he told me as we walked together for what seemed like the longest. "But before I ever let you get on, you gon' have to learn some lessons about the game. First, keep your enemies close and your friends closer. I know most people say it the other way 'round, but in this line of work you can't trust anyone, especially not your friends and family. Secondly, I don't care what you get exposed to; remember loose lips sink ships and could cost me everything, including my life." As Coolly Lee talked, he had a real gangster stare in his eyes. He wanted me to know the seriousness of the business and after watching him for some time, I did. But still, I knew deep down selling drugs weren't my thing, I had an itching for lifting and was determined to make that my thing.

During the next few years of school I'd spent less time

focused on what was happening inside the class room and put all my time and effort into the streets. I mean, don't get me wrong, I did try to win over the educational system, but was gravely disappointed. When May 2000 rolled by, I'd still, despite attending school until the very end which was more than I could say for the rest of my boys, ceased to make it out with any type of qualifications worth progression. For the first time ever I felt robbed and although still deemed a child I knew that I'd acquired more skills on the streets to make me successful than I would in any class I'd attended. I left school without enough grades to get into college and I refused to retake my GCSE's, sixth form was out of the question. Education just held me back, sitting in a hot ass class all day when I could have been lining my pockets with cash. Each day I'd watch my step-mother and father leave for work only to obtain a pay cheque that lasted a little over a week. Yet each month they'd continue their ritual as if they hadn't learned from the month before. I just couldn't live like that. I'd had a taste of what the streets had to offer and was determined to get my share.

For the first few weeks after leaving school, I found myself sleeping through the morning because I simply had nothing to get up for; my step-mum made it her point to give me the "You need to be doing something with yourself" talk from the bottom of the stairs each and every morning before she left for work. Most days I couldn't tell whether Klinton had a pulse or not. Since school, I'd long earned the respect from my brother's friends around the estate while he slowly began to lose his way. I'd watch Klinton and his friends smoke skunk roll-ups. Then as everyone got older, I accompanied them to raves where the music would change from Reggae to Jungle, that's where I noticed the high demand for the "E" tablet (ecstasy). I saw people who were naturally coy and tamed turn wild and erotic once the intensely pleasurable effect had taken over their bodies. There was no age limit to these raves as I can recall rolling through an advent called Splash in Homerton that only charged five pounds upon entry from as young as nine. Drinks were eighty pence and I always managed to get drunk off the cheap Shandy cans. By the time I'd turned fourteen the estate had gone crazy. Almost all the Olders were smoking crack cocaine; it was like the 'It' thing to do. They called it "The rich man's drug" because it had a knack of becoming an expensive habit. Klinton often came home both drunk and high beyond belief covered in the stench of his own vomit. Many morning's I'd be up getting ready for school and I'd be unsure whether he was dead or alive. His eyes just a blank stare and his chest barely moving to indicate breathing. His mum would throw a fit when Klinton, who was almost always too wasted to make it to the bathroom, would bless her carpet with his intoxication from the night before. After a few months of his unpredictable mood swings, she had had enough and contacted her parents in Barbados, pleading with them to accommodate him until he returned to this normal sober self. I remember thinking, *Lucky bastard,* the morning he left for the airport. His excessive drug abuse had become so out of hand that he was wanted in the streets for all sorts of things such as petty theft and unpaid debts. People had even gone as far as to approach me in regards to his whereabouts, making it clear that if they couldn't find him they'd kill me instead.

My father and step-mother were oblivious to what was going on in the streets. Either that or they didn't care. They showed no sort of compassion towards me what so ever I was receiving threats from home.

"If you nah go do nuttin' wid ya life you carn stay inna dis house," my dad had said to me a number of times. To him, England was the land of opportunity and failure was not an option. A simple minimum wage job would have been acceptable to him, but that wasn't enough for me. I wanted more. The constant nagging had me wanting them to kick me out I was convinced that them kicking me out would be just the push I needed to complete my transformation to street thug.

"You know, if planned properly we could have robbed over a hundred yardie's and been rich by now if, you know if we hadn't wasted all that time in school!" I'd vented to Greek's in the early hours of the morning. Because like me, he hadn't done any better and was still broke.

"I hear dat', brov." He yarned and stretched. We now had to find some kind of hustle to keep us a float. We both had reputations that we had to uphold. Both Greeks and I came from homes that on the outside looked great, but only that close could see past our deception. Greeks had been brought up by his Gran, a woman whom to date is the loveliest woman God could have put on this earth. She'd always treated me as if I was her son and no one could tell her otherwise. She didn't want to hear it. She was one of the only people growing up that made me feel that there was a good side to me and my life.

Having looked after Greeks since he was a baby, she became his mother. Greeks never grew up not knowing his real mum, though. In fact, we were all familiar with his mum. I'd always assumed that the pressures of life was too much for her to cope, so she turned to alcohol constantly trying to drown out her past memories.

Staying out as late as we could to prevent going home as the streets were full of fun we both became full-time employees of the streets. If we were bored, we would walk to another area and rob some drug dealers. There was no way we'd miss any opportunity to make money when the streets had displayed its treasures in plain view. At fifteen we became crafty street robbers, often targeting the rich and the wealthy in different boroughs.

"What you saying about Islington? You still on that for tomorrow?" I asked Greek's as I relaxed on the extra mattress his Gran had bought just for me for the nights that I stayed with them.

"Yeah, course I'm on it," Greeks answered without hesitation. "You gonna let me ride, right?"

"Course!" I mumbled, reaching under my pillow where I kept my mobile phone at night. In the life we were beginning to live there was no such thing as time. You were a slave to your mobile phone. Once it rang, you moved and without it you were as good as dead. Greeks was excited about our plans for the day. We'd decided a few nights back that them white boys in Islington was gonna get us through the summer nicely. Two men strong we rolled up on them and robbed them for their bikes, which were stolen. That was their thing. They would steal motorbikes then in turn use the bikes to do smash and grabs in the city. We'd watch them for weeks before school broke up. The driver would pull up next to a jewellery shop to allow the passenger to get off and with a silage hammer shattering the glass; they'd try to grab as much jewellery in as little time as possible before riding off back to Islington. They were well-organised because they came from long generations of gangsters. Their fathers and uncles in the same area had passed down the technique. I knew deep down they thought of killing us because after a while they knew we would wait for them to go into the city and rob bikes so we could rob them. But there was nothing they could do about it. We'd ride around Hackney on their bikes pretending to girls that they were our own. At that moment dealing drugs was too much hard work. While money was our motive, we were both content and satisfied with the rush we got from personally robbing and assaulting an unsuspecting victim.

CHAPTER: SIX |

Me and Greek have remained tight throughout the next few years that followed. He wasn't the best fighter on the block, but he never lost any of his show downs because we had a pact. All he had to do is give one punch and I was in there. We would stamp out the other person to the point where Greek's was known around Hackney as a serious guy, one not to be messed.

We were best friends and would die for each other. My mattress at his Gran's house meant I could sleep there nights in a row. We shared a true brotherly bond.

Greeks cousin, Smithy and I, on the other hand, were never best of friends. He always felt that he was better than me and Greeks. He was shorter than us and I guess that made him feel like he had something to prove, like his height gave him status. He was a sweet boy, the kid all the girls around the way liked. Light-skinned, with a fresh hair cut. In school, Smithy always had new trainers and a jacket, while the rest of us hood bound boys would get a new jacket and trainers every four months. That is if you were lucky.

Now Smithy and Greeks' mums were sisters from the same mother, but they chose different paths in life. I can't tell a lie Greek's Gran would try her best, but life was hard. Back in school, Smithy would tell the teachers how he didn't need to be in no shit assed class because he was gonna become a big time drug dealer like his older cousin L Smithy. Smithy lived his life trying to be like L Smithy. He even named himself 'Junior,' which to him meant next in line. For a while Smithy had me convinced. Sure enough after we graduated from school, L Smithy finally gave into our pleas of wanting to become big time drug dealers. He gave us an eight ball of heroin, just one up from the smallest amount you could buy from a distributor to sale. It was enough for us to make a start. We both hit the roads hard trying to round up drug addicts who were reliant on the stuff. Our aim was to build up a contact list on our mobile phones. We called this "our line." The more contacts we had, the quicker we got rid of our supply.

After a week I had gotten rid of all my stash while Smithy was on his third round. I knew the drug game wasn't something I could see myself doing for the rest of my life. So I met up with Greeks and with the money we had between us we bought a car and started driving around seizing the opportunity to rob anything and everyone in sight.

"Yo! Roderick. Get your ass in this whip (car)" I shouted from the driver's window as I sported my new car through Stoke Newington estate.

"What, is this you yeah Que?" Roderick asked excitedly admiring my new ride.

"Yep." I said looking at him through the rear view mirror with the biggest grin on my face. Roderick was one of my best friends on the block so it seemed only right that I allowed him to benefit from my good fortune.

"Rah, you lot are on point," Rod pounded Greek's then me before getting out the car. I'd given him a lift to the high road.

"You know how we do" Greeks said.

"Yeah, you man are ballin." Rod laughed "I'm out." he said before he walked the small distance from my car to the shops. I watched him before I pulled off and made a mental note to keep in touch. On the streets you never knew which road life would take you down, I was getting money, whipping it (driving) and doing my thing. But I also understood how hard it was watching another man from the same block eating and living nice when you were still struggling.

By the end of that week Greeks and I had more money than the drug dealers in the area. That's when Smithy decided he wanted to join our robbery operation. But he was sneaky and would wear tracksuit bottoms under his jeans and would drop money down his legs before we shared the money between us. I found this out on the night of one of our biggest robberies.

"How much you think in here?" Smithy asked once he and I were alone in the car Greek's and I had bought earlier that month. We had a recently stolen safe in our possession and sat waiting on Greeks return, as he'd gone to get rid of the car we used in our crime.

"I don't know, but I know it's a good couple of grand in there, 'cause it's fucking heavy," I remember saying before seeing that look in Smithy's eyes. It was like I heard it before he said it.

"Come; let's take a couple hundred before Greeks gets back." I couldn't believe what I was hearing and I was sure the expression on my face stated that, but Smithy still went ahead stuffing a few fists full of notes down his pants. I was in shock. To think we brought him along with us and we were getting robbed. He was robbing us and still making money from his drug dealing. I just had to get at Greeks. And I did Later on that night, I told Greeks what had went down and it was decided that Smithy couldn't be trusted.

"Que!" Greeks called my name, bringing me out of my thoughts as I checked my missed calls and messages. I smiled because I had two missed calls from my boy, Snaps, and I knew exactly why he'd been blowing up my phone.

"You gonna let me roll wid da bike, yeah? Cause I got some gash (girl) I'm gonna link in the evening. She wanted me to link up with her today, but she ain't from the ends and I ain't trying to get caught slipping like some dick-head, ya hear me?" Greeks cheesed as I thought about my own plans for the day.

"Yeah, I hear you, I gotta get some credit and holler at Snaps 'cause he trying to get me on this chick that his tings staying with for the week but she lives in the ends so do your thing."

"You gonna roll with him to the chick's house?" Greek's asked almost shocked.

"Yeah. Why?" I raised my brow. The many robberies we did attracted a lot of attention from the opposite sex, but like I said before, I was never interested in having a "girlfriend" like many of my peers. I was determined to stay focused, that and the fact that girls, in my mind, were a complete waste of time. Yet, it was that summer I met Renee and my accusations regarding relationships were confirmed.

***

"Yeah, I'm coming, but why you really want me to follow you?" I asked Snaps, one of the local boys I'd become fond of. Snaps was from a street gang I'd become more involved in since leaving school. He was from Queens Bridge road, which sat directly across from Holly Street Estate. Being from Stoke Newington, I had to take a trek through Kingsland high road to accompany my peers, but in more ways than one it was worth the walk. Most of the Holly Street members were students at Homerton Boys' School, so a lot of relationships and bonds started in the playground. Others who lived on the block thought that gave them authority, and made them leaders. But it didn't. The Olders were always in control and by 1998 everyone who was anyone in Hackney knew about the Holly Street Boys. There were so many of us that on any given day there could be up to twenty of us on the block at one time. Talking noise and most of the time disturbing the peace. The Holly Street Boys were like a family. Life between us became simple for most, and many of the members who joined in the early years. Like a brotherhood, what you'd do for your blood brother, you'd do for your bredren [Brethren]. It was impossible for another gang member from a different set to stop and interrogate one of ours without the whole crew jumping in. It was the same if you were caught slipping in another ends. If you got hit, the whole crew would be down to do whatever it takes to avenge you.

"Cause I told you her friends gonna be with her and she's gonna need some company init." Snaps sarcastically explained. I closed his front door securely behind me and followed as he led the way to our destination. I knew Snaps was planning on using me to occupy his link's friend while they entertained each other. I just wanted to hear it for myself. Snaps had always been cocky, quick at the mouth, and always had a story to tell, but he was weak. To date I couldn't tell you of one person who'd fought him and lost.

"Cool man, Trust me, she's your type. My ting is gonna be staying with her for the week. And her parents are almost nonexistent, it's cool." Almost in a begging tone Snaps tried to convince me to tag along.

"How you know what my type is?" I turned and asked him, half laughing because I was trying to think if I even had a type.

"Come on, Que." Snaps chuckled. "You like light-skinned girls, right?" still laughing he asked as we crossed over to Richmond Road.

"Yeah but so do you." I quizzed.

"Exactly, everybody likes light-skinned girls, that why you gonna be feeling Renee. Plus she's cool and she's local," he said before he held his finger down hard on her buzzer.

"Hey Snaps!" Sharleen came running to the door and greeted him with a kiss, which at the time I thought was funny because this was their second interaction. She already knows what time it is. I smiled to myself.

Sure, Sharleen with her tight waist and slender figure was pretty enough, but something about Renee caught my eye. Snaps was right. I was feeling her.

"So what school did you go to?" Renne asked. She sat next to me when Sharleen and Snaps departed to the family room for a more appropriate setting for their antics. Renee was short, rocked the classic hood gel-slicked back ponytail with the sweeping fringe hairstyle and gold hoop earrings. She had light brown eyes and a dimple in her cheek. Overall she was cute and I didn't mind her company.

"Homerton. Why?" I played along with her twenty questions. I was trying my best to keep up the conversation, but for the most part my mind was racing over-time, thinking of the things I could steal from her house. I must have scanned the room twice over before deciding to call it a long shot.

"Ah, you might know my cousin then, but he was a few years above you," she continued, proud of her discovery.

"Who's your cousin?" I questioned, keeping up the banter.

"Coolie Lee!"

I literally saw the name roll off of her tongue. Suddenly I was really feeling Renee.

"Yeah, I know him," I stated, proud but cool. I wanted to be like him so bad I let my guard down and started warming to Renne. We talked swapped numbers and promised to keep in touch.

"What you think about her? You think you gonna link her?" Snaps asked me later that day as we walked back from Renne's house.

"I don't know." I shrugged.

"Well, did you at least get her number?" Forever cocky, Snaps walked along side me like he had grown ten-inches taller since he'd left Sharleen's side.

"Bruv, I ain't gay. Of course I got her number." I felt myself tense up.

"You should have done your thing then," Snaps said as we reached his door. "You coming up?" I shook my head no; I wasn't feeling his attitude and knew that if he continued to talk to me the way he had been doing today, I would have him laid out in the street gasping for air.

I walked to the top of the road, crossed over at the crossing, and made my way home, my second home. The block. Long gone were the days when I hung out in Stokie (Stoke Newington). My new spot was Holly Street. Home. Becoming a gang member of the Holly Street Boys made life simple for me. Their reputation made it safer for me to go through different parts of the borough because in most cases once you left the security of your estate you're out there alone and vulnerable. Our generation represented post codes, the E9, the E8, and the N16 and so on, defending their territory like lions. Again, everyone in Hackney knew what us Holly Street Boys were about and knew not to mess with us. We put fear into people, fear that could last a lifetime and fear that also brought love. I thought about Snaps and how he'd sarcastically spoken to me that afternoon then smiled as I got closer to the block. Being in a gang brought the feeling of having an alternative family. It provided a feeling of belonging, but also delivered fake love. Most boys on the block would have your back in a fight while others were just there to make up the numbers. They would never get involved in the wars that our lifestyle created. They always had an excuse why they couldn't fight. We knew who the real soldiers were from the very first gang fights we had.

CHAPTER: SEVEN |

It was late afternoon when I reached the block. The sun was still shining and the ends was looking good. All the pretty young Hackney girls that would often would travel from post code to post code trying to link up with someone from each crew had us as the talk of the town and they were jamming with us night and day. Normally, I'd call someone in the morning to see what the plan was for the day, but we always met up in one of two spots, outside Malcolm on the other side of Holly Street or Smithy's house.

I acknowledged my boys as I posted myself against Smithy's wall.

"Wass up." Smithy waved me over.

"Cool," I said, we gave each other nods between the conversation and laughter, which I soon found myself getting into. They were talking about the London Fields Boys and their status in the hood. Smithy had centre stage.

"Nar dere' gay. Real talk, they out here making P and everybody knows bitches love P." As spokesman Smithy referred to the lack interest the Field's Boys had when it came to the females and he had the rest of us in stitches. "Yet, they ain't getting any pussy. It's cause they don't want it." He shouted the last part and we all fell out laughing.

"I bet you those faggots are gonna try something stupid this week!" I said, referring to the unplanned weekly sparing matches we had without fail. It would kick off when one of us would punch or CS gas one of their boys. Then because they'd always loss they would cheat and round up their older brothers to jump us. Plainly because they knew our Olders weren't into warring over bullshit.

"But they getting fucked up if they come into our ends again." Smithy joked, causing laughter between the crew again.

"Yo Mark. Lil Mark!" My boy, Trav shouted, spotting one of our boys in distress coming from the direction of London Fields. Trav was well known around the hood and had proved to be one of the most loyal members of the crew. If you ever got into it with someone and needed to even the score, Trav was down.

"Come 'ere, brov. What's good?" Trav asked Lil Mark with deep concern.

"I just had a fight wid dat bitch, Paperboy. He fucking punched me in my eye," he said, still panting and holding the side of his head.

"Come, we go find dem?"

"Oi!" Pepe, another well known member of our crew rounded up the gang. There was no way we were gonna take this laying down. Lil Mark was one of us. If you insulted him you insulted us all and we weren't having that.

The post code for Holly Street is E8 and London Fields is E9. Just separated by a single road it's almost impossible for a person not to need to cross lines, but for the most part we'd made it possible. They had the Mare Street McDonalds and we had the Dalston Mackey D's. We had our parks and leisure centres and

56

they had theirs. Was there any need to cross the line?

Fifteen minutes later, we were walking across Queens Bridge road to London Fields. By the time we got there our twenty man strong crew had turned to twelve. We'd lost eight men on the way. I guess the fear and the reality of the fact that we were going over there to cause a mini-riot was too much for Pepe. He was one of the first eight that ran off before we got to London Fields. He would always talk the talk until it was time for action.

"Where the fuck you going, huh?" Trav said as we ran up on them Fields Boys. Each of us was on one of theirs. We got down and dirty in minutes. It was on. Hands up, it was the first and the best gang fight ever in Hackney to this day. No guns, no knifes, just your fists and your feet. Even Orion, Trav's friend from school that he'd known from nursery days came to represent and he was from Tottenham. For the simple fact that he was always at Trav's house and he was like mandem (one of our boys) to us. Putting in his all, he was fighting twin brothers and he was winning. It looked like he was delivering a thousand punches and that shit looked good. I didn't care about the effect it was having on the twins. Orion, he was on my team. I was there doing my thing and I looked up for a breather and spotted Trav on the grass fighting another two boys. The boy I was fighting, Eddie-P was getting wounded until his older brother stormed over and gave me a big right hook that shook my brain differently. I immediately stopped pounding his brother because I didn't want another one of those "big man" blows again. We were going all out, giving it our all. Lil' Mark wasted no time taking out his frustration on any one of those Fields Boys that he could get his hands on before Trav's phone started ringing.

"Hello," he answered it. Both us Holly Street Boys and Fields Boys paused for Trav to continue his call to what sounded like his mum.

"Yeah, okay. Yes Mum. See you later." He hung up and the rumble continued as if it had never stopped. Orion continued beating up on the twins while the rest of us continued to go buck wild. If anything this was the day to prove your 'realness' and your 'gangster.' Events like these have earned a select few the respect we still possess today.

CHAPTER: EIGHT |

On a typical Friday night in the hood, everyone would link up around ten. A hour or two before we left out you hit a club. No matter where you were outside of London selling drugs or robbing people we would all link up and take our position. Four cars one in the front new the direction of what club we was going the two cars in the middle would have the guns in and the cars in the back would stay behind not letting no one get behind the cars with the guns not even the police. If needs be we would have to block off the police so the cars holding the tools could escape. We had to stay tooled up because we were always raving out of our comfort zone .We were bosses and when travelling out of town and entering into another gang zone we had to be prepared for trouble.

"You can't get past this frame without getting searched!" a guy who looked to be about two hundred and fifty pounds blocked the entrance to the club with but arms folded to his chest. Usually we would bully ourselves into a club but there were often times when the bouncers wouldn't have it.

"Boss, they know us. Ask that man over there." Coolly Lee pointed to another bouncer who was busy searching another party goer.threw Renee, Lee and I had become close and hung out together on a regular basic.

"I don't have to ask anybody shit." He said defensively "If you don't want to get searched move to the side," he then continued to settle the crowd of eager ravers ignoring our presence and dissing the whole crew.
Mr. two hundred and fifty pounds seemed to be new at his job; it was obvious he didn't know what time it was or even who we were.

"Fuck all this," I said making my way through my boys to front of the club "Where's Gary?" I asked.

Gary a tall built bouncer turned around and smiled, he came my way and greeted me before proceeding to let us in the venue.

"Hey, G. What you doing man. These boys ain't been searched and they refused for me to do so when I asked. Man you know the rules." the first bouncer again tried to stop us from entering.

"Whoa, B. Their cool. We don't want any trouble let em in." Gary spoke up noticing my boy Lamont reaching under his shirt.

"Fine. Let em in." Looking from us to his colleague the bouncer shook his head and continued with his job else where.

"Thanks G." We all pounded the loyal member of staff before entering the club. Some of us still held some feeling towards the way the first bouncer had dissed us at the door, especially because he did it in front of a slue of females.

Inside the clubs the vibe had us hyped. Girls that's usually wore tight jeans and T's that their legs and breast on show while the club owner sent a constant flow of drink our way. His way of keeping us sweet so we kept the peace in his establishment.

"What's happening?" I asked a chocolate coloured girl as she flashed me a smile and pressed her breast up against my chest making her way past me to the bar.

"Nothing." She shyly answered.

"You want a drink?" I asked her knowing she'd say yes and open up.

"Yeah, Jack Daniel's and Coke!" She shouted over the music. I nodded and ordered her drink before noticing the ignorant bouncer from earlier making his way through the club.

"Here, hold on." I told Ms Chocó, handing her the plastic cup containing her drink not once taking my eye off the bouncer. I followed him through the crowd ducking behind people when he looked over his shoulder. I had him cornered when he went into the gentlemen's restroom. Standing over the stall he retrieved his penis from his pants and began to urinate.

"Tough guy yeah?" I grabbed the man by the back of his neck and threw his head forward sending him flying into the wall in front of him.

"What the…" was all he managed to say before I'd grabbed him again and sent him flying into a cubical where he landed on his ass, his dick still hanging out his pants.

"I can't leave you alone for ten minutes can I?" Coolly Lee came through the door shaking his head, startling me.

"Get you fat ass up." He shouted to the bouncer who now sported a nasty gash above his left temple.

"Come we flush him." Lee turned to me and laughed, he was wasted off of alcohol and weed while I was sober. This was to be my high. I rolled up my sleeves and tussled with the bouncer as he tried to break lose of the grip both me and Lee had on him. Trying to turn him over was a mess; he thrashed his head violently in the water in the toilet bowl before I lifted him up for air.

"Plea……" he splattered before I dunked his head in once more.

"TUNE!" I turned around to see Lee doing a two step to a new joint the DJ had just put on. I let the bouncer go, washed my hands and followed Lee out onto the dance floor. That will teach him I smiled to myself as I watched my boys enjoying themselves. The incident in the restroom had me hyped adrenalin ran through me like a bolt of lightning, I pictured the bouncer struggling in my grip as I plunged his head into the toilet and remembered how he'd pleaded for me to stop. Tonight had been a success I'd undoubtedly installed fear into a grown man and would be leaving the club with his Rolex, gold chain and a new camera phone from the handbag of Ms. Chocolate who now occupied the dance floor.

At two-twenty-eight in the morning, Renee lay in her bed waiting. She knew I wouldn't get to her before the streets were empty and all the local hustlers were safely tucked away at home. That was one of the things that kept me into her. Fifteen and already lost in the streets, I dug the fact that she just let me do me. Her older sister and mum whom she lived with thought she wasn't old enough to have boys over, so it was convenient for me to sneak into her house at this hour of the morning. Hooded up, I tapped lightly on her bedroom window and seconds later she was at the door. We'd tiptoe upstairs to her bedroom.

"I love you so much, Gwenton," Renee panted into the night while I slobbered and kissed all over her neck and collarbone. I knew this was what Renee wanted when I'd come to see her. As we kissed, she'd unfastened her night shirt and let it drop to the floor. Guiding me to the bed, she unfastened her bra and suddenly she was naked. I wasn't a virgin before Renee I'd had sex a handful of times with an older girl on the block. Still, I would rather rob people because after sex I was still broke.

"Put it in," she begged. It was sexy when she said that, but I hated it. I did as I was told and gently guided myself into her moistness giving her what she wanted. She wanted me to please her and I wanted her to be okay. Besides Coolly Lee and a few other distant cousins, I was the closest thing to a male in her life and I guess she wanted to be loved by at least one.

"Yes, Gwenton!" Renee whispered as I grinded inside her. We were way past the fingering phase and although I wasn't keen on the feelings love brought, I loved the feeling of being able to satisfy. "I'm cummin. Yes, Gwenton." I held her tight, pounding into her tunnel until her body quivered and she collapsed on top of me drenched in our own bodily fluids. It had been three weeks since we'd met and I still wasn't comfortable cuddling after sex. She'd started referring to me as her boyfriend, calling herself Mrs. Que. I just went along with it, telling myself we were just good friends and any type of relationship we had was all in her head. I wasn't looking for a girlfriend, but as Renee lay cuddled under my arm I knew I couldn't just abandon her. Renee's home life was quite similar to the lives of most young girls that lived in high crime and drug constituted boroughs. Her mother was a single parent to multiple children and struggled financially. There was no father figure in her home, the effects causing Renee to crave security and stability. Something that my reputation preserved me to be able to provide. I wanted to look out for her, but deep down I knew I couldn't. I had my own problems at home and her vulnerability was no match for my growing love of the streets.

A man with a powerful street presence can be both a blessing and a curse on a woman in love. Love in the streets means pain. Everything has its price. A hustler has the potential to provide a woman with a life of luxuries and hood fame, but as a consequence the life he lives requires him to step on some toes in order for him to remain at the top of his game. Just one disagreement can cause his whole operation to fall back in times of war, making the people around them his enemy's next prime target.

Revenge is delivered in many ways in the streets, but what's worse than killing your enemy is murdering someone they love. When a woman gets involved with a man in a gang she immediately gains a place in his downfall. There are many ways a female can become a target as a consequence of being in contact with a gang member, but the unfortunate part is that while the man might know this he may never tell the woman. A classic case of denial, him believing his status has made him untouchable.

Ladies, the term "gangsta in the hood broken down means

"gang-star." Gang: Being his crew members, his boys. If loyalty is tested it's these people he'd risk his life for as their love for him in the streets prove that they would do the same. Star: Being the incriminating reputation they've built on the streets.

What may seem like a simple favour could mean your life; giving him a place to sleep for the night, driving him places in your car, letting him use your car. The man you have sleeping in your house could have just committed a serious crime. You could be driving him away from the scene of a crime or he could be using your car to commit a crime. How you explain that in a police interrogation saying, "I didn't know nothing," will only get you a one way ticket to prison.

I felt Renee's dead weight on my arm and looked at the time on my phone. It was something to five in the morning and I wanted to at least be home before the street lights turned off. I slipped from up under Renee and positioned her gently on a pillow covering her naked body up with the quilt. The house was still except for her mother's snoring bouncing off the walls in the flat. Quickly I got dressed and let myself out. *Is a relationship worth all this baggage? Feeling guilty and being responsible of the lives of others?* I thought to myself as I bopped down Queens Bridge road en route to Kingsland high road. I wasn't into using girls nor was I into loving them. My childhood had shown me good love and bad love. Although half way into my teens and quite aware of wrong and right I wasn't accustomed to either. Tired and frustrated for the rest of my journey home, I tried to remember the love my mother and father shared, but it was hard because it had been so long since I'd seen them together. Suddenly my thoughts strayed to my mother, the only person I'd truly ever loved. Yet there was so much I hadn't told her. Finally, I made it home and put my key in the lock. My step-mother had put the latch down in an attempt to keep me on curfew. Her rule was if I wasn't in by 10PM then I wasn't coming in.

I only had to ring Greeks once and his Gran's door was open.

I went inside and collapsed on my mattress into a deep sleep where even in my dreams I struggled with love and why it brought pain.

I dreamt I was back in Jamaica with Keisha outside in the humidity of heat on the Island play. Keisha was a skinny, little, brown-skinned girl that lived next door to our family in Jamaica with her twin brothers and mother and father. We were both five and could often be found playing together in the yard with dirt and stones as neither of us had any toys. Well one day while Keisha and I were playing in the dirt and searching for bugs, her mother called her into the house. She told her to go to the shack-like shop up the road to buy a small bag of rice amongst other things she needed to prepare that evenings meal.

"Gwenton, mi affi go ah shop. Ah soon come, yea?" Keisha shouted coming out of her house and walking in the opposite direction from the yard. I wasn't allowed to leave the yard when my mum and dad weren't home, but I didn't mind waiting. In fact I had no other choice; Keisha was my only friend for a mile. I waited for her around the back for a little while. Then when I got bored I ventured back around the front hoping to see her coming back down the hill, but I couldn't. With no sign of Keisha and hunger growling in my stomach, I made my way back to the house to find something to eat.

Most days like this it was just Faye and I at home. She'd cook for me, clean up after me, and most days entertain me from the early hours of the morning until it was time for us to go to bed. Faye was my best friend, but so much like a mother that I was growing tired of her bossing me about, telling me to go play in the yard and to stop running up and down the house.

"No, stop it," I heard Faye say, followed by a giggle as I got closer to the yard door. I barged it open to find Dante, one of Keisha's older twin brother's squirming around on top of my sister trying to pull down her jeans. I didn't think. I just remembered grabbing the broomstick from behind the door and swinging it hard, lashing Dante right across his bare ass.

"Ahhhhh" he screamed out in both shock and pain while Faye tried to cover up that what was exposed of her body.

"We were only playing, G," she tried to explain in a frantic voice, but I wasn't trying to hear that. With my broom in hand I chased Dante back through the fence and watched him return home wounded before I went back into the house. I felt like giving Faye some lashes of her own for trying to sleep with my best friend's brother. I thought about the look on Dante's face as he desperately tried to unbuckle Faye's jeans and wondered what it was that Faye had that he wanted so bad. For days after that, I'd presumed Faye had done something wrong, but it wasn't long before both twins took turns braving it over the fence, leaving me no choice but to tell Keisha what I'd seen her brother doing. Then she told her mother and one night as I slept I listened to the sweet sounds of a beating, knowing that I wouldn't have to chase those boys off our yard again. That will teach you, I smiled to myself. No one comes into my yard when I'm here. I flexed. I still wanted to tell my mum what my Faye had done to be certain it wouldn't happen again, as she didn't seem amused at the beat down happening next door. Lucky for her, I couldn't stand to see her get disciplined therefore I didn't tell our mum and neither of us spoke another word of Dante, his brother or the fence.

CHAPTER: NINE |

Home was like a battlefield and most days I preferred to be on the streets. My step-mother and I were in continuous disputes regarding my rough lifestyle and the lack of respect she claimed I had for her house. But she somehow managed to show compassion on the morning I got an unsuspecting phone call from an aunt on my mother's side of the family, urging me to make contact with my mother. She was now in England and in bad health and it was suspected she didn't have much longer to live. I was livid. It had been seven years since I'd heard news of my mother and to be told she didn't have long to live was a blow to the heart. All the feelings I'd hided inside for so long began to surface and I began to feel rage come over me. I remembered how growing up in Jamaica was hard, almost everyone I knew there was working to survive and often relocating seemed to be the only way forward. Out there is nothing like the way life is in England. In England is possible for you to have dreams to buy your own home or a nice sports car. But in Jamaica a parents dream for her child is his survival, to make sure your family wasn't starving. I could understand why my mother would agree for me to permanently reside in my father's care but I dint understand why my father would allow my step-mother to have a say in how we communicated in her absence.

I felt robbed. My father and his wife had robbed me of loving my mother; I could have been taking care of her when she needed me the most.
When my father heard of her poor health he was gutted, I could see it in his face although he showed no emotions I knew his heart like mine had skipped a beat and was hoping just like me that she would beat her illness and pull through. I couldn't lose my mum, not again.

I didn't know any of my mother's family and so I waited a whole week before a meeting was set up and I could see my mum. All kinds of thoughts went through my mind during that time. I was in an uncomfortable position wondering how my mum would look as the message my auntie Jean left was that my mother's was in a really bad way.

During the months commencing my mothers' death, I grew bitter and cold. Instead of the greeting I'd received from my father's mother back in 1992 .My mother's mother was vile and untouched by her daughter's ill state.

"I don't want you to cry when they lay me to rest, Gwent. I want you to be strong so you can look after your sister you hear?" my mum would say reaching for me each time I visited her, her health showing no improvement, even on her death bed she remained proud and strong. I hated to see her like that but I was grateful to see her because while she needed me, I still needed her.

"I don't want you to die" I fought back tears.

"Everybody gan die, Gwenton, but it's how you die that matters." It was hard growing up without hearing the words "I love you" from a parent or even receiving a simple hug. I treasured each and every moment I spent with my mother before she passed yet nothing could prepare me for her death.

It was just another day on the block when me and Snaps retired to his house joining his mother and sister around the table to eat. There were very few houses in Hackney I felt comfortable eating in, but Snap's mum's food was real good, plus she treated me like family.

"Mmm this looks, good Mum." I said, just about ready to dig into my mounted plate when my phone started ringing.

"Faye, what's up?" I answered seeing my sister's name flash up on my screen.

"G, mum's gone in a coma. You need to get down here. Now! I'm calling a cab for you."

"What?" I let out followed by an excessive amount of questions that I knew my sister didn't have the answers to. In a bid to get me off the phone Faye took down Snap's address then disconnected the call after demanding I go to the front and look out for the cab.

"You alright Que?" Snaps followed me down the stairs as I made my way to the front door and opened it. I felt myself inhale the cold air sharply then I stopped breathing altogether, not saying a word. No tears fled my eyes nor did any wails exit my mouth. I waited for the cab in silence and when it arrived I got in and closed my eyes. What was wrong with her? Why my mum? Is she gonna be ok? I asked myself over and over again, not ready to let her go.

I last saw my mother on a Saturday in the hospital where she'd been for the last month or so. Her usual healthy frame was now skinny and frail as she had now stopped eating and refused to be fed anything offered.

"Gwent, come eat this for your mum." She stretched out a weak arm towards me, offering me an apple pie someone had given her earlier in the day.

"I don't like apple-pies, mum. You eat it." I said shaking my head. Faye had just left the room to use the bathroom and my mothers' eyes pleaded with me to eat the damn thing. For my love for her I would have eaten a hundred, but what I wanted more than anything was for her to gain back her strength. *At least then she would have a chance,* I'd say to myself when I thought about her current condition.

"I'm ready to meet my God now, Gwent." she fought back tears and said, "Tired of being a burden on my own mother and family. It's embarrassing. I need to be free, Gwent." She reached for me as Faye returned to the room.

"Please, mum, you have to start eating you know what will happen if you don't." I went into what the doctor had told us that morning hoping that that would change her mind about her attempts to starve. I left the hospital that day pleading with my mum to eat or else the doctors will have to feed her through a drip. That was just three days ago. I should have known when my mum said she was ready to go she meant it. She was a woman of her word, one who lived and died by it.

When my mother died and was laid to rest, it somehow felt unreal. I wanted to curl up into a ball and not think about it, Let sleep take me and allow me to forget for just a while, but I couldn't. My sister needed me and I needed her too. To me my mother's funeral was the end of a hard life for her and the beginning of a troubled life for me. I would never love another soul besides hers. Though there would be a time for tears, a time for the nearly crippling pain of loss, I knew that time wasn't now, not yet. I have to keep it together; I told myself each and every time I stepped out into the cold grasp of the streets. But it was hard with the constant memories intruding my thoughts . . . her smile, her voice, her comforting words telling me everything will be just fine. I missed her dearly and would do anything to have her back.

My mother died in 2001 from cancer cells that spread through her whole body like a forest fire. She was told of her condition less than two years before she passed and was subjected to months of consistent pain in which nothing seemed to help. I miss her more than I can explain and while I haven't yet accepted her death or grieved for my loss, I've acknowledged the fact that she is now at peace, without pain and no longer a burden on the people she called family and friends.

Now almost sixteen my mother's death brought out a more sinister devilish nature in me. I wasn't as close as most would think I should have been with my dad and sister, but then every family's different. While myself and Faye attend her funeral and comforted one another I refused to allow my father to attend. I was angry, and my only thoughts were *He didn't serve her any purpose when she was alive. What could he possibly do for her now.*

Throughout my life I've lost other family members and friends through violence or accidents but none of their deaths really rocked me as losing my mum did. Her death created a void that I doubt I'll ever be able to fill. I loved her. Because she is Mommy, and she wasn't supposed to leave me before I got married and had kids. I thought I had more time left with her and still I continue to thank her every day for showing me how to be a man at such an early age. She is my inspiration and I still get weak when people that know her say to me, "Your mother would be very proud of you." I love to hear that because that's something I know I ill never hear her say again.

Emotionally I was in need, and was never the type to abuse my body with alcohol or narcotics, but I needed someone. Being an adolescent I reached out, but nobody reached back. Friends didn't know what to say and for a while even my step-mother tip toed around me until she decided enough was enough and everything should go back to normal. I tried to get close to Renee but I just couldn't respond to her love. It had been two years since we'd first hooked up and I was ready to bring what we had to and end.

"I'm so sorry Que, I. I... I don't even know what to say." Renee put both arms around me and hugged me tight when I broke the news of my mothers' death to her. She's had been blowing up my phone something crazy the last couple of weeks and although I was hurting I knew it was only right that I gave her and explanation for my absence.

"It's okay. You don't have to say anything, I'm cool." I slipped out of her embrace and flopped down onto her bed.

Renee began kissing my neck and at the same time whispering how sorry she was for my loss saying things such as; "I'll always be there for you Gwenton, if you ever need someone to talk to, you know you can talk to me, right?" I closed my eyes as Renee made a move for my lips.

"What have I done, Gwenton?" she asked when I refused to kiss her back.

"It's not you Renee. It's me" I tried to explain but she began sobbing holding tight onto my arm.
I tried to loosen her grip. "I can't do this with you right now Renee I got too many things going on right now. I know I should have told you sooner but I want us to be friends."

"No, Gwenton, I need you. Why? What have I done?" Renee wasn't hearing me.

"I can't be your friend. I need you, and you're all I have," she begged. It hurt me to see her like that and although I'd endured more heartbreak than I could take, a small chunk broke off each time she begged me to stay with her.

"Listen!" I turned Renee around and held her face in my hands. "Chill with my boy, Eugene for a while. He's cool and we can still be friends, I promise." I said feeding her a line, hoping she'd get that I wasn't into the relationship thing but I still cared.

"You gonna do that for me?" I asked, rubbing her face with my thumbs.

"Okay." She sniffled, easing off me then wiping her tears with the backs of her hands.

I later hooked Renee up with Eugene. They seemed to hit it off until I later learned that during sex he'd invite other boys to sleep with her much to her discretion. I was hurt. To ease the pain I returned to the streets. I now held down a major position in the Holly Street Gang with a fast growing reputation as the guy for robberies and gang fights. I was keeping good company in

Pembury Estate too with Green-Eyes, Poops, Pepe and Lamont. It was at that time I met Kat, a man fourteen years my senior, willing to go to war with me side by side against people my own age. It was my good friend at the time, Pepe, who introduced us to each other, but word on the streets was that he and Lamont were cousins. Back then I played it cool. I'd heard good things about Kat in the streets and once we started to hang out my whole outlook on life changed.

Kat was five-feet-seven with big, beady eyes, light brown skin and his hair line had started to recede, but other than that he was cool. He made it look cool to be in a gang. It was "Death before Dishonour" with him and "Do or Die", "Get down or get robbed." He was more like an older brother and he dressed like us and spoke our slang. Kat would never be seen without the latest gear. During my mid teens I spent most of my time with Kat, watching the way he spoke to his workers with authority. They listened. *I'm gonna be like that*, I thought, observing how he brain-washed the whole area post code by post code *I'm gonna be like that.*

Kat schooled me on everything I needed to know about putting in work and staying safe on the roads .Never let your right hand know what your left hand is doing. Over the years we became close, and hung with each other every day. He would come to my house I would go to his and that was big for him I was one of a handful of people who knew where he lived, you can't just trust anyone with the whereabouts you lay your head. Especially with some of the things he told me he'd done to people in the past. We were making enemies by the day. Robbing people was his thing also and he taught me everything he knew.

Kat had the connection for anything you needed and if you didn't need it and imagined you might need it, he could get it, within a matter of days. I'd always wondered if had a link to a private jet, but deep down I didn't care because when I reached out he reached back. We got into clubs free from Old Street all the way back to the West End. We rolled through like the old school white--

gangster's you grew up hearing about. Kat was in so deep that I can recall a time where we'd met up with a member of the notorious Adam's family because he needed one of their workers robbed for his work (drugs) in order for him to remain in their debt. Kat knew I loved robbing drug dealers. He must have seen that twinkle in my eye because he gave me that hit, which turned out to be one of the easiest robberies I'd done so far.

"You know what time it is. Gimme your food. We're going back to your house to get the belly!" I sternly told the small blonde boy who claimed to be in his early twenties.

"Come on, mate," he whined. "My mums gonna go spare if I bring you up in my house," he pleaded. I guess he didn't bring many of his black friends home.

"I don't give a fuck! Get your ass in there." I shoved him, showing him I meant business. I wasn't into disrespecting peoples mum's at the time, so I didn't step foot in the house, but the tone in my voice and the look in my eyes told old boy I wasn't playing.

"Okay, all right." He held his hands up like I was gonna rob him in the street. "Just let me go inside and I'll be out in a bit."

"Ten minutes," I said sternly.

"Okay, ten minutes. I'm gonna leave the door cracked so you know I'll be back," he said as he disappeared into his house. Within ten minutes he returned with a plastic bag full of money and chopped up cocaine in lottery tickets ready to sale.

"You know who I work for, right?" he asked with a slight grin before handing his belonging over to me. "The Adams family won't be happy to hear you robbed me"

Yeah, I laughed to myself thinking if only he knew that it was The Adams family who put me on him.

"They got any problems, tell 'em come to Hackney. They'll find me," I said unfazed before I made off having done what I'd come to do.

I was always getting little move's like that. Every day there was someone or somewhere to rob. Someone wanting their partner

74

to get robbed or an ex-girl friend seeking revenge.

Kat and I would go to the Spiral Mint Rhino strip club and drink champagne most nights complementary of the bar. It became our thing. At the end of the night we'd collect our earnings. We got paid for making sure there were no disruptions between the customers and staff. Kat taught me to do nothing for free. We lived freely, partying in The Embassy Club where all the up and coming stars would party. We hit other clubs like Aquarium, 10 Rooms, and Browns. I was never into drinking and getting drunk. Instead I spent my time in the bathrooms. I stole watches, chains, you name it. If it shined it was mine.

My mornings were a quick trip to the local pawn shop. Although most of the time the joke was on me when I found out the things I'd stolen weren't real and didn't even come close.

"How much does your chain and watch cost?" I asked Kat one day when we were in the safe house after another hard night grafting at the club.

"These old things?" Kat turned his wrist to catch the light on his watch. "Don't worry about all that right now Que," he smiled "You can't buy things like this you have to earn it." Kat smiled wider, inviting me into his world.

CHAPTER: TEN |

The transition happened so fast that I almost couldn't believe it, but it was real. I'd grown out of the whole Holly Street Boys phase and was now a member of a notorious gang that had been established in Hackney since the early 1980s. LOM (Love of Money).

Under Kat's authority, LOM controlled parts of Hackney's drug distribution with a strong hold. Kat wasn't the original leader I later learnt that he'd been playing front man while the original boss was serving a long sentence. Being front man, Kat would rob whoever was making money in the area, all the drug dealers, local hustlers, gamblers, other robbers, but never people doing nine-to-five as they wouldn't hesitate to go straight to the police.

By now I already had a name around Hackney. Everyone my age group knew I was not a guy to be messed with, but now I had personal problems with the main players in the ends The Fields Boys were still holding it down in E8, except now they were causing mess in Tottenham. They were known for getting all the other gangs in Hackney caught up in their beef with the Tottenham Man Dem (TMD). The result of that was the TMD yout's coming to Hackney and trying to kill whoever they could find, not knowing that the people they really wanted were the Fields Boys. I constantly had sparring matches with the Fields Boys over altercations I'd had with the TMD, but eventually it became a routine, something I and everyone else learnt to live with. The Fields Boys had Olders who were well known, serious guys who didn't mess around. They had all types of weaponry, bats, crowbars, guns you name it. They were always at war with the TMD. Well-respected drug dealers or bank robbers, they were only about making money.

Kat was like the answer to all my dreams. He, like me, was fearless and he detested the Fields Boys. I don't know if it was because they all had money or if he needed us to join him to keep his name ringing because all the other old school gangsters who were in their 30s were either in prison or on drugs or washed up. Me and Pepe were ruthless members of LOM. With Kat behind us we would party anywhere we wanted, crossing post codes and enemy lines. We had the connect for guns and food (drugs) and Kat would bring us in on at least one Robbery a week, we were making bigger names for ourselves while lining our pockets. We were untouchable and I was loving it, I was at a place in my life where I was on top. People showed us love where ever we went. I was swollen with admiration for Kat much so that I was completely thrown back when my good friend Lamont was murdered.

A genuine ladies man Lamont Tyrone Silcot AKA Monty grew up in a house full of women. He seemed to understand the females while they stayed trying to understand him. Unfortunately the Fields Boys made his life hell until one day he decided enough was enough and started to fight back. He was now down to do what-ever it took not to be a victim again.

One night on Carpenters Road, Monty and another ex member of LOM called J were hanging out of the window of my new car putting work as I drove past Club Space, a night club situated on the back road. On route we spotted one of the Fields Boys that had shot after me the week before. I could still see it in my head as if it were yesterday because that was the first time I ever saw Monty perform.

"You're dead, pussy. I swear you're fucking dead!" Monty shouted busting his strap out my passenger window. J had the back window covered while Kat was tailing behind us in his brand new MG two-seater with a Mac Ten refusing to overtake us. Monty's death shook me mentally.

Lamont was killed on a Sunday at 7 PM, on September the 19th 2004. As he sat outside his girlfriend's home in his mini Cooper, an unidentified vehicle pulled up with their lights on full beam blinding him as he tried to identify the driver and his associates. Straining his eyes, Lamont didn't stand a chance as the driver exited his car and crept up towards Lamont's car, and shot him in the head.

Lamont was killed instantly, leaving behind a grieving mother and brother and two sisters who loved him. To my knowledge the reasons behind Lamont's death are still unclear, there had been a theory around the time of his death that some of his old friends that at the time were doing time for a murder put a hit on him from jail so they could blame the murder on him another theory was said that he was setup to be killed to send a warning massage to Kat.

Was this the lifestyle I really wanted to live? I asked myself after hearing of Lamont's death.

***

When someone close to you dies, you automatically put yourself in their place. Thinking about all the people you would leave behind had it been your time to go. You'd appreciate them more, and let them know how much they mean to you incase you never get to tell them again. It gets like that on the roads. Your boy dies or you witness someone close to you get killed. No matter what type of illegal hustle you're involved in there comes a time when we think *That could have been me.* I've thought that many times. And that's what I was thinking then, at that moment whilst I was still grieving for the lost of my mother and now the loss of a friend I wanted to be close to home. To spend more time with my father. My step-mother and he detested the fact that I was preserved and stereotyped as a gang member and on many occasions made it clear that they wanted none of it in their home. My step-mother's protests were more frequent since she claimed she paid all the bills in the house. I tried to create peace at home but it wasn't long before the monster in me was provoked.

"Nah, I can't stay here for you lot to keep chatting your madness in my ears," I vented with much attitude and no remorse, voicing my opinion to my step-mum who sat with her head in her hands at the kitchen table.

"Don't worry, I'll be cool," I assured her as she sniffled. "Why are you crying? This is what you wanted, isn't it?" I raised my voice and held my hands out as an expression.

"Gwenton, sit down. Don't leave, when your father gets here we can talk, all of us." This was my step-mum's attempt to beg me to stay, but I had already made up my mind. I thought. This is what they wanted. I was filled with hatred for the both of them, walking around the house on a daily basis like a living, breathing, ticking time bomb. My mother had just died and I was blaming everyone around me, especially my dad and step-mother, for all the wrongs they'd done to her and even more so for stopping our contact at a time when she needed me most. If I knew she was dying I could have sent her money to see a proper doctor. Maybe that would have given her more time. I looked back at my step-mother, who seemed to be in a state of distress, seated at the table with her back hunched and streaks of tears running down the side of her face. I left her alone and slowly made my way to my room.

Long gone were the days of me and Klinton sharing a room. Even with him in Barbados I refused to mix his belonging with my own.

"Something, something, something." I heard Joyce murmur through her cries. Although I couldn't understand what she was saying, I sat on my bed packing not paying her much attention. Vexed I packed my clothes and a few cassette tapes into the only bag I owned with my mind set on moving in with Faye.
It was things like this that made me wish I'd had the chance to leave sooner. My bedroom was about 4x2 between the kitchen and the front door. Neither my step-mum nor my father had any objections towards me occupying such a small space. A heated surge of rage went through me when I thought about the many times I'd had to play off my friends self invitations to my house for fear of them finding out my bedroom was our old freezer room.

Fuck it, let's just get this over with, I said to myself, hearing the jingling of my father's keys as he entered our small flat. My ears followed the sound of his footsteps as he made his way to the kitchen then perked up when I heard both adults engaged in a dispute.

"Carlton, you need to talk to him. His really getting out of hand he told me to get the fuck out his face today." My father called me into the living room. I strode in there with my bag on my back mind already set on making my departure.

"I've had enough, Dad" I raised both my hands and my voice "I can't have people thinking they could talk to me any how I'm not a kid" my father looked at me strangely, but I didn't expect him to understand. We both stood in silence and I took that time to study the man before me. Carlton Sloley is an opportunist; he always had a plan and is one of the smartest men I've come across. He could hold his own in a conversation of any genre from politics to the streets, and despite our differences, he'd always given me advice on how to keep safe on the streets, such as schooling me on loyalty amongst friends. I could think of at least twenty times his teaching had gotten me out of a tight spot, yet his teachings were rare as I'd long suspended myself from his lessons. I loved him undeniably, but if I didn't leave now our relationship would be ruined beyond repair. I'd watch his gambling on horse's progress, growing into an unsustainable habit that could have easily put us out on the streets. My step-mum, now his legal wife by marriage would punish me when her husband failed to meet his parental demands and cuss me out saying that I should be grateful for all she's done for me growing up in her house.

"Your father doesn't contribute shit. This here is my house and you are living with me," she'd say, making sure I was aware of her; status in his life. He needed her, she was carrying him. I didn't want to be a burden to any woman let alone my father's wife.

"Where you ah go stay?" Dad asked me, watching me shift where I stood. Surrounding us was a place that had brought me much pain and although I hated to admit it, my father had administered it. *Could things have been different if I'd come to England to live with my father alone?* I asked myself before looking over to my step-mum, I thought of my mother struggling until death the only mother I've known in England had contributed to my unhappy childhood and had failed me as a parent.

"I just don't like him touching my things," I remembered hearing Klinton say when I'd first arrived in England.

"It won't be long, son!" I couldn't get those words out my head.

"I'm going to Faye's. She's gonna let me stay with her." I tried to sound optimistic although the situation at hand was breaking my heart. I left that night not happy but content, I called Faye.

"G, what's the matter?" Faye asked like she'd sensed something in my voice to indicate distress.

"I'm fine, Faye. But I need a place to stay." I said quickly calming her down.

"Why? What's happened."

"I can't stay there right now. Can I stay with you?" I asked her whilst I made my way to her house. There was no doubt in my mind that Faye would say yes. I knew she wouldn't have her little brother sleeping on the streets. It had been a while since we had hung out but I guess our mothers' death had brought us back together. Reunited us even.

When I was six Faye moved out of our home in Jamaica and found refuge in a young girl's home. I always wondered why she moved out and left me, and then I later found out that she had made claims that my father had touched her sexually as a child and for her own safety, she left the family home.

"How far are you now?" Faye sighed.

"What you don't want to see me?" I joked "You don't want to see your little brother?"

"Shut up G. Just hurry up and get here. Have you eaten?"

"Nah," I said trying to remember the last time I ate. Greif does that to you. Steals your appetite and determination. It can take away the very best of you and it leaves nothing but time and pain.

"Okay. Well I'll get us a pizza. See you soon" Faye disconnected the call.

Apart of me was relieved. What if I had blown up at my step-mother house and things got nasty? What if Faye hadn't agreed to let me stay with her? I was kind of glad things had turned out the way it did, I had maintained my composure and respect and wriggled myself out of a potentially bad situation. My father, I would always love, and as for Joyce, I have buried my only mother.

CHAPTER: ELEVEN |

At first living with Faye was cool. We spent most of our time chilling together in her place or hanging out with her friends that not surprisingly didn't even know she had a younger brother. We got on great at home too. We'd keep ourselves occupied and pretend that our mother's death wasn't and hadn't affected us until I couldn't take it anymore. Back in Jamaica as young as I was, I knew Faye and our Mum didn't get along. Whenever they were in the same room with each other there was some sort of breakdown in communication. It would always end with Faye screaming at the top of her lungs that my mother's father, our grandfather, had fathered her, and my mother was a bitch because she wouldn't admit it. I spent a lot of time struggling with the skeletons that had come out of my family's closet since my mother's death. Whilst living with Faye, a lot of things that neither I nor Faye would have liked to admit was true came out of the wood work. Often, it had me questioning the day we laid our mother to rest.

Listening to everyone talk about how "Gwendolyn Hamilton was loved by all" angered me almost to the point where I considered walking out of the service. Why? Because I knew what they were saying was all lies. In death her silence was magnified.

Sobbing on my pillow I recalled my findings for five years. During my mother's childhood her own father sexually abused her, impregnating her in the late 70s and abandoning her as she gave birth to Faye. He threatened her with the consequences of other people's opinion if she spoke out, so she would often make up random people to blame for impregnating her. How I was uneducated to this growing up is a mystery as everyone acted as if we were the perfect family. Me, my mother, father, and Faye. I did not find out about the sexual abuse my mother was subjected to until she was on her death bed. Even then she refused to admit Faye's father was her own for fear of disappointing her own mother and causing gossip amongst other family members.

To hear this with my own ears was such a shock to me that I was sent into a deep depression. The thought of some dirty old man raping my mother tortured me. I was back to my old ways wanting to kill and not fearing fate I broke with all reality.

Because quite simply, I realized that my reality was a lie, a deliberate lie crafted by my parents and my grandmother.

If my mum's death wasn't enough to deal with at sixteen, it had been brought to my attention that my sister was the product of sexual abuse subjected to my mother by her own father. I was livid. I had never met my grandfather but just couldn't understand why he would want to sleep with his own child. My mum was fourteen years old at the time, around the time normal school girls are having their first boy friend or crush. I wasn't naive but didn't want to believe all this could be true.

"Our father. Your grandfather regularly invited his friends to the house when our mum was out. I even caught a man in her room once, but when I told my mum she dismissed it and gave me a beating. I was too scared to speak out after that. We all took it as a warning. We knew what was going on but was scared of the consequences if we spoke of the things we'd seen." My mother's sister explained my mother's painful past. I was full of anger with no one to hurt. I wanted to kill someone. In the streets I was Que. I would kill someone with no questions for a member of my gang, much more the person raping my mum. Slowly, it all started to make sense why my mum packed up everything she owned, gave up her flat, and left England when my sister was seven. She was running away from home.

This was all too much for me to take in. I couldn't get my head around all this new information. My sister was now also my aunt what kind of family is this?

After my mother departed her family home, and after she recovered from the abuse from her father, she dedicated her life to the church. Covering up the past and pretending that everything was perfect. The problem is that now we are a family which focused only upon the surface of things. None of us really knew each other. I sat in the church at my mother's funeral, and realized that I am a stranger to her side of the family. Pretending like they knew her, like they were lifelong friends. I was angry and hurt. Angry that people cared after my mother's death and hurt that my grandmother couldn't have been honest and protected her daughter. That was the second family secret to be laid on the table. One more was to come out during this time.

Although Faye was ten years older than me, I was her brother and my duty as a male was to look after her. That and the fact that I was respecting my mother's wishes.

During my stay, I would do robberies and give her cash, not all the time, but small sums now and then. I wasn't a "bad man" or a "gun man" nor did I want to be. I was a "robber man" and with that reputation comes people trying to challenge you. So I was always ready to perform and drug dealers were my favourites. If you sold drugs in Hackney I would try my best to find out where you slept, who you slept with and what your phone number was to try and get a lead on you by one of your customers. I was friends with a lot of girls at the time, and either through heartache or spite they almost always had someone to setup. It could have even been a guy they had slept with just once before but had had a keen eye and knew where he kept his money. I've always said that a woman is the most dangerous person after your best friend when you're living on the streets because some men pillow talk with girls in the morning or after sex. Just the feeling of excitement and anxiety makes a lot of men let their guard down.

Months went by and Faye was as cool as I was with the set up until her dude she was dating at the time started coming around acting like he was man of the house. I could tell they both wanted me out and tried my best to stay out their way I understood grown people needed their space. My lifestyle kept me missing for hours, but it didn't work out. Tension emerged between us so much so, that one night I returned home late to find that she had locked me out and refused to open the door.

"Come on, Faye. Open the door!" I shouted wrestling with my key in the lock. After ringing her bell for a good fifteen minutes I suddenly remembered I'd left the kitchen window open. So I walked up the road, climbed over the fence, and jumped over five gardens before climbing through her kitchen window. I was tired from my activities during the day and headed straight to the bedroom to sleep. From the corner of my eye as I walked to the bed room, I could see Faye hiding in her front room pretending like she didn't hear me at the door. That night I laid in bed thinking, how could my own sister lock me out? I would have left that night, but had no other family I could ask to stay with. People don't mind you staying a night or a weekend, but nothing more. Faye's actions hurt me. If I was the crying type my pillow would have been soaked, but I'd learnt to cry internally and was a master at keeping in the pain. The next day I left Faye's house I knew I wouldn't be getting back in that night. But I couldn't risk the chance of staying in and missing an opportunity to make money. So I took all the cash I had and a change a clothes not knowing where I'd be sleeping come night fall. I left my bag and a speaker at Greeks house, too proud to tell him I was homeless.

That night I made my bed in Dalston Kingsland train station. For the first few hours I'd jump up every time a train went by then I got tired. Why did Faye let me stay with her? Out of pure guilt. As I settled into my makeshift bed on the side of the overhead station, I thought back to Jamaica where the line between brother and sister was crossed and in my opinion the core of my child hood was lost. Finally, as the station became deserted, I placed my hands in my jacket then curled up in a ball with my hand between my thighs. Fatigue hit me like a ton of bricks and before I knew it I was asleep.

***

I couldn't have been any older than five because I remember at the time fiddling with the small plastic buttons on my shirt, wondering why it was so hard for my little fingers to push the damn things through the holes. But I was independent and adamant that I'd get them in. There was no rush and nothing else I had to do so I took my time, listening to the heavy rain outside beat down on our zinc roof. I fiddled and fumbled in the back room getting dressed while Faye sat on the bed in thought. We'd spent most of the week inside the house together alone. As usual our mum and my dad would always be at work. They worked all hours of the day, leaving Faye in charge and me under her authority. Faye didn't have any friends that lived near our house so we would often play together despite the ten year age gap. I would play with her dolls, as I had no toys of my own, and would sometimes pretend to be a girl. Faye would comically dress me up in her clothes.

I'm doing it, I'm doing it. I slipped one button at a time into each button hole, proud of my accomplishment. "Look Faye. See what I did." I walked across a pile of sheets that had been left unfolded on the floor and crossed the room to where she sat.

"See!" I straightened my shirt. *Why she looking at me like that?* I don't know when I lost my footing but I did. Faye had pushed me onto the bed and was trying to perform an act of which I knew only grown-ups were allowed. We exchanged no words, just pain, as Faye touched me searching for an erection to give her satisfaction. Stiff with fright and confusion, failing to understand the reason for my sisters actions of betrayal. *Maybe she was going mad. All the fights and arguments between mum and dad had rubbed off on her and now she's trying to kill me,* I thought with my eyes closed. Unable to watch as Faye continued to get my body to obey to her body's commands. I knew what she was doing was wrong and I was scared. For years I tried to block these thoughts out tried to hate Faye, but I couldn't. She's the only person I had left with my mum's blood running through her veins.

I awoke.

"Next train to Richmond calling at 06:35. Please mind the gap when boarding the train." I'm in the train station, damn. I rubbed my eyes ready to make a move to my next destination. I gathered my belongings, a small bag, half a can on KA Caribbean cola, and a packet of mints. A few days ago I was driving past homeless people on the streets, sleeping rough and begging for cash. I always thought *How could a man lay down his pride and ask another man, a complete stranger for money?* I was no longer searching for the answer. Straightening out the clothes I'd slept in, I cringed at the thought of having to spend another night in the station. The lonely, cold nights made it easy for you to hate the world and everyone in it.

All I have is myself, I thought as depression sank in. With my bag on my back I made my way to the exit walking past the yellow line close to the track. I pulled my phone out my pocket. Not one missed call. Almost contemplating, I wondered, *Would anyone miss me if I jumped in?* Lost in my own world I was ready to do whatever it took to survive, but I wasn't ready to go home. I phoned Trav.

"Wah-gwan, Que? You good, yeah?" he answered on the third ring.

"Nah, my sister kicked me out this morning," I lied. "I need a place to stay. Things are fucked up at the moment," I started to explain.

"Say no more, bruv. I see you when you get here, bless." He ended the call. I put my phone back in my pocket and put some heart in my step. It was then that I knew Trav would remain a true and loyal friend. He was accommodated in a hostel for young homeless teenagers and if caught with another person living in his room he could get evicted without notice.

We kept a low profile, me staying with him for just under six weeks. He soon swapped his hostel for a one bedroom flat in Bounds Green just outside Wood Green, giving us the freedom and space to expand our crimes. Trav was down for whatever. With both of us holding down our Holly Street Boys reputation and me repping LOM, we were falling deep into the gang life, so deep that the word on the streets was that it was just a matter of time before one of us ended up getting killed. Our new independence found us seeking revenge for all wrongs that had been done in the past, from anything as small as a dirty look. Until suddenly everyone around me was catching a case.

One Friday night me and Trav, along with Core a fake cousin of mine travelled to a party in Edmonton. Core lived in Edmonton and was only respected because everyone in his area knew we were family or at least he was pretending to be. I had the power, he had the brains, and he knew how to make money playing poker online. He would use other people's credit cards to buy chips to play online and he had recently hooked me up with my new girl, Charlene, who was best friends with his girl, Charlotte. So we hung out quite a lot. In fact we were always together.

Trouble was in the air. I could smell it from a mile off as we made our way to the party and got closer to the location; I looked at the crowd and didn't like what I saw. It was like a Tottenham gathering. All the big names were there, even some we thought were in jail. We were a bit taken back at first, because we also started to see Wood Green boys coming out of this club. It was strange because we thought the two areas that were at war were partying together. Me and Trav laughed. Were they all friends when no one was looking?

We were cool with the boys from Wood Green because most of them went to school with Trav. I also knew many of them through my friend, Stilts, who was their leader. I'd done moves with some of them in the past Trav and I got a bit relaxed and started talking to a few of the Tottenham boys' girls'. They always loved us Hackney men, calling us gangsters and gentlemen. They were all over us then the next thing I knew, all hell broke loose. I don't know if it was Trav or Core, but I just started punching people's faces off. I was known for my right hooks I felt like I was in a western. Me and Trav were back to back fighting the whole road. We had tools on us, but didn't really need them because we were winning. But I guess Trav got bored and decided to put an end to the easy fighting.

"Oh my God. He's bleeding." A girl screamed out from the crowd.

The next thing I saw was a light-skinned boy holding his side and then he was on the floor. That was the only time I saw Core back us. Me and Trav looked at each other and knew we had to get out of there, so we ran back to the car wondering if the boy on the floor was okay. We waited for phone calls from the girls that were there watching. All we had in our ears was Core asking if we saw his two kicks and punches he gave the guy as he was on the floor.

"Shut the fuck up." I chuckled, causing Trav to laugh. We were still worried about the guy who had fallen, but we would wait to hear the talk from the girls that were there watching. Girls are like news-paper they spread news fast. The way I saw it they started it and we just defended our own.

"Fuck, imagine what would of happen if we took all our tools," Trav said when we were back in our own ends kicking it in my car.

"I don't know. I don't even wanna think about it, but I do know that for the next week we better track down all the people we were fighting one by one and seek revenge for the disrespect of challenging us."

"Yeah, course," Trav agreed, and true to our word we did. We drove around every area in Tottenham trying to find the people on the wide list of names we were given, but no one wanted any trouble. At that point we felt like we ran Hackney and. Tottenham I would later leave Trav to face a court case for stabbing the light-skinned boy during our brawl. I couldn't understand it; I was sure they started the trouble with us. Why should they have the right to go to the police? But again that's the way it goes in the streets. Sometimes the people that get hurt are the trouble makers.

CHAPTER: TWELVE |

In 2001 there was a noticeable gap in each and every gang that Hackney had given birth to. Most members who were locked up were enduring long sentences for armed robbery, violent physical attacks, drug distribution and murder. They were considered lucky compared to their friends whose lives had been lost.

I moved through Hackney building friendships, making business connects and committing crimes. I went from Stoke Newington to Pembury estate. Holly Street to Jack Dunning in Homerton. Homely Estate in Stamford Hill kicking it with the Rowdy bunch and LOM. I even ventured as far as Brixton where I met Elijah. I watched Elijah turn his life around taking his loyal friends with him. I was still caught up in the roads when he decided the street game was a joke. He gave it all up to go legal, I admired his strength. It was a big risk he put his life on the line to make the change. Those who knew Elijah would call him to the ends rob the older Hackney boys they were at war with. Elijah was the man for the job. He didn't play around and most the time he didn't even come strapped, he had a knockout blow that was enough to do the job. We were young guys robbing big men. I knew he was respected in his area but I wouldn't know the extent of his popularity until much later.

I was always moving with a different crowd. Kat and I hadn't hung out much during the last year. The older men who still associated themselves in gangs had a knack of disappearing for a while. Whether Kat was tucked up for winter with his latest squeeze or keeping a low profile our friendship was one where we would give each other's space to breath, but we would always meet up to discuss business that couldn't be spoken over the phone.

Moving back home in the summer, I spent most of the winter Kicking it with Green-Eye, Cherrie, Tempa, Risky and Poops. Members of The Rowdy bunch who today are call SOS (Straight out of Shakespeare) because a majority of the member's lived on Shakespeare estate.

"Blood, where you going?" Green-Eye randomly said as we took a stroll on Dalston high road. I turned behind me to see him grilling two London Fields boys who despite being on our turf had the audacity to be grilling him back.

"What you doing in our ends, blood?" I snatched one of the Boys College passes from around his neck and read his name out loud, intimidating him. I wanted him to know that I knew who he was, and I wasn't going to forget.

"Come man," the shortest boy said "We go Shoreditch college, how we gonna get there without cutting through your ends?"

"Huh?" I looked at Green-Eyes who looked at me, quite surprised. On our territory the Fields boys were out numbers but these two were trying to be brave.

"No answering back, pussy." Green-Eyes smacked the boy who had just spoke in his mouth, bursting his lip.

"Fuck you!" His friend spat and began throwing punches, one of which caught me on the side of my face. I was mad, and could tell from the look in their eye's that they wished the ground would open up giving them an underground tunnel that lead them home. But today they was out of luck. We battered the two of them there on the high road. Green-Eye punching up the short guy and me tussling with the guy who's punch had caught me in the head. It was personal. As he balanced on the curb I punched him in the face, then lifted my leg kicking him in the stomach and into the moving traffic.

The boys stumbled onto his feet then froze as the driver of the bus approaching slammed on his breaks, saving his life.

On October the 4th I planned on hitting up one of the clubs we controlled in the West End for my 19th birthday. I wanted to celebrate it big, champagne, VIP and sexy girls. That's how we did it in the hood, flossing our cash and getting swollen off the haters was what we called a good night out.

"Yo, where you lot at?" I cheesed down my phone. The plan for the night was that Green-Eye, and a hand full of other guys was gonna link me at my dad's house before we went out. Maybe open a bottle of champ's before the rest of the party rolled through then we were out. I was on a buzz.

"Open your fucking door. You Muppet." Green-Eye laughed "I'm standing outside"

"What's good? Birthday boy." Marlon playfully punched me when I opened the door and stepped out.

"Look at you doh. Fuck me!" Green-Eye studied my swag. I wore a blue Nike puffer jacket with the matching bottoms, they had a white stripe running down both arms and legs and I completed my look with a blue NY base ball cap and black Nike leather gloves. The gloves were to install fear in any enemies I would come across tonight. Just encase I'd have to perform, my finger prints would remain out of police evidence. As a finishing touch. That was what we rocked back in 2001.

"Brov. Stop gassing him." Marlon said swigging on a red bull as the rest of the mandem showed up in an entourage of tinted out cars blasting their music with bass. We drove through Stoke Newington to Upper Clapton where we slowed down when we approached Clapton pond.
The night club Palace Pavilion opposite the pond.

"Oi, Oi. Que." Green-Eye tapped me on the shoulder and pointed out the window.

"I swear that's the dude that set my Audi A3 alight."

"Lemme see." I leaned forward and looked for myself. "Yeah, that's the little prick right there."

"I beg you come we move to him." Green-Eye said already unbuckling his seat belt. Everybody was hyped and on a vibe for my birthday. We all agreed and parked up, then made our way across the road to the club.

"Sharon!" I called out running ahead of my boys. I knew that Sharon worked behind the bar and wouldn't be searched re-entering the club. So I caught her before she went back in and put a proposition to her.

"What you saying, Que?" Sharon swayed her hips my way. Sharon was the typical hood grown West Indian chick, nice round waist with a firm behind that made her jeans look painted on.

"How you mean?" I teased her, pulling her towards me from the crowd of party goers waiting to get in the club.

"When you gonna come see me?" Sharon placed her hand on her hip, licked her lips and asked.

"You know it's my birthday right? I looking to handle some shit and be out. You should roll with me tonight."

"Aww. Happy birthday." Sharon sang "You want me to roll with you for real though?"

"Yeah, course. Why not?" I said peaking over her shoulder. Trying to see where my boys were at and what the current situation was.

"You know. You're with your boys, and I know you got a girlfriend. People gonna talk"

"Yeah. So" I put my hand on Sharon's waist and brought her towards me.

"Look. Ain't nobody gonna say nothing when your rolling with me. But look" Sharon touched the pendent on the chain I wore around my neck and smiled. I looked over her shoulder again and Green-Eye was calling me over. I held up my index finger One minute he knew what I meant.

"Hold this for me." I whispered in Sharon's ear as I discreetly placed my tool under her top, touching her skin. I felt Sharon shudder then covered her as she hid the tool in her clothing. It wasn't uncommon for a man to approach a female he knew from around the ends and use her to carry his weapon encase of an emergency.

Scanning the club full of young ravers for the wannabe arsonist, I caught up to my boys with Sharon by my side greeting the familiar faces from the hood. Palace Pavilion occasionally ran under eighteen nights.

"What's good, Que?" A younger from one of the sets I ran with greeted me with a pound.

"You cool yeah?" I replied as bobbed and weaved through the dance floor. "Oi. You seen them Stamford Hill yout's?" I asked the young kids, who were following me.

"Yeah. Dem pussy's are up in the VIP." he pointed to the upper level.

"Safe for dat." I said. Looked over my shoulder and spotted Green-Eye. "Look. See dem idiots over there?" I put my arm around Green-Eye and pointed up to the VIP section.
Like snakes in the grass, Green-Eye and I snuck up to the upper level and joined the VIP party.

"Where's this fool?" Green-Eye growled growing inpatient. Girls purposely bumping into us would have been a delight had it been another night, but we hadn't come to party. I looked around the small red velvet and black upper section blocked off as the VIP, with the black leather sofas and glass tables and couldn't for the life of me spot the dude who had set Green-Eye's car on fire.

"We fucking lost him. Let's get out of here." I raised my voice so my boys could hear me. Palace Pavilion was old school to me now and I didn't plan on celebrating my birthday with a bunch of hype and unstable kids. I felt like a man.

"Let's roll." Marlon said as we turned back down the stairs making our way back to the entrance.

"Nah. Wait. I swear that's his friend over der." Green-Eye said pulling me back into the crowd.

"Fuck all this. I wanna bounce." I huffed "What's the point with fucking with his friend, when he ain't got shit to do with shit."

"What! Man burnt my fucking car. You think I'm gonna let him get away with burning my shit. Come we fuck his boy up. Show that fool what is like to see something that belongs to you damaged."
I could have fought harder for the little dude but his warfare wasn't my concern. For once I wasn't in the mood to get into a madness. I wanted to enjoy my birthday, so pulled away from Green-Eye and told him I'd wait outside. I walked slowly down the stairs, holding on to the banister. Paying attention to the atmosphere around me, I noticed that some of the girls I'd earlier dismissed as I'd entered the club were on their phones. Giving me guilty looks and whispering amongst themselves. Something isn't right, was what ran through my mind.

"Brov. Let me hold these?" I asked a young boy I'd seen from my block. Without waiting for an answer I took the sunglasses he wore and placed them on my face, then I picked up a couple of flyer discs to hide my face.

The cold October air stung my face as I stepped out the club into the night. I felt for my tool, feeling it against my skin kept me at ease.
Should I wait here for dem man or should I wait in the car?fuck it. I told

myself not wanting to be caught slipping in such a bait spot. I braved the cold and took a right onto Clapton high road where I froze; wishing I'd followed my initial thought and waited by the club.

To my right had to be what looked like no less than ten London Field's boys, waiting in the alley way with intent. They spotted me immediately and my eye instantly caught the figure of one of them bent on his knees pointing a piece of steel in my direction. I'm about to die. My heart raced uncontrollably. Okay, calm down. I told myself. There must be a way to get out of this. Every second I spent stood in the spot I'd frozen in could have been my last. I couldn't go back into the club because the bouncer had already closed the door for the night, but I had one thing left up my sleeve. It was a long shot but I was willing to try anything if it meant me living to see another day.

"Ahhhhh" I screamed at the top of my voice, waving my hands in the air like a mad man. I ran straight towards the gun man and continued past him, throwing him off his aim. I know once I was on the other side of the road I'd have to continue running because although I'd been able to put him off his aim there was nothing stopping him from firing at my back.

"Bang, bang, bang." I heard the shots being let off behind me. I was running in zigzags, something I'd seen on the TV. It was a known fact that bullet didn't bend corners. As I ran I looked over my shoulder and saw what looked to be ghosts speeding towards me, and only missing me by chance. I reach for my side and felt for my piece, I had only just remembered I was armed.

"Aguh." I grabbed my left hand. After I'd pulled out my tool and cocked it back. I'd been hit. A surge of pain shot though my left arm. "Aguh" I was hit in the back of my left hand "Fuck their coming to finish me off" I spoke in a whispered to myself as I grabbed the back of my leg and struggled with the pain. I saw a slew of boys racing across the road towards me. I had to do something. I pointed my gun at the crowd of boys, manipulating the situation and as I did so I heard shots ringing out behind me.

Green-Eyes had come out the club with his guns blazing. At the Fields boy's. I continued in the opposite direction, in pain. Ashes formed over my bloody wounds with each step I made. I need to get to the hospital.

I slowed down just by Mare Street and caught my breath when Green-Eye and my boys rolled up beside me I got into the car. I was hit but I wasn't down.

"You cool, Que" Malcolm asked me, moving over to make space for me in the backseat.

"Yeah, I'm alright."

"What the fuck happened?" Green-Eye asked, driving away from the hospital.

"I told you I was going outside. Next thing you know I got LF (London Field's) on my back. Where we going" I was kind of pissed off because for one it was my birthday and I'd be spending it in the hospital and second, I'd made it clear in the club that fucking with that dudes boy was a waste of time. We should have all left out together, stuck to the plan and we would have been in West by now. We didn't go to our local hospital to get me cleaned up. Green-Eye drove us all the way to the city. By now we knew that the police would be all over the club, people would have been questioned and news of me being shot would have gotten around. We couldn't take the risk the Field's boys coming to finish me off while I was laid up in a hospital bed.

"Blood. Did you think you were in a movie or something? Why didn't you just run?" Malcolm asked me once we were inside the hospital and I was banded up. I found out that night that I hadn't in fact been shot but I'd shot myself, when I'd panicked and cocked back my tool I accidentally let if off injuring myself. The bullet that hit me in the hand just grazed my skin but because of the swelling it looked as if the bullet was buried deep in my flesh. I was still in a lot of pain but I had my life.

***

"Trav. What you doing here?" I sat upright holding my hand as Trav came into my room the next day. I was released from hospital that very night. I didn't wait around for stitches or to be bandaged up, I cleaned myself up.

"What do you mean? I just heard. I had to come see if you was alright. You know that girl that lives in my hostel?"

I nodded yes.

"Yeah, well she was at the rave and she saw everything. I got to the club as soon as I could. I thought you man might have still been there"

"Nah, us man. Got out of there. What's it looking like?" I asked wanting to know how the scene was looking. I hadn't noticed before but Trav's clothes were ruffled and he wore a frustrated frown on his face.

"The place is a mess. I was two minutes away when I heard about the shooting. I spoke to a few girls who were hanging around outside the club and they said that the shooters were long gone." I already knew that.

"You good doh?" Trav asked me, concerned.

"Yeah I'm fine. It's nothing." I held up my hand. I respected Trav for putting himself out there like that, coming to have my back even if it meant putting himself in danger. Trav didn't tell me at the time but I later found out that some boys from out the area had tried to rob him for his chain.

I kept thinking about what had happened and what would have happened had I been hit somewhere critical. It's easy to clown with your friends about what you would do if you was put in that kind of situation. But until you have really been there you will never know what choices you have if any.

I still lived with these memories, which I had put to the back of my thoughts around that time I became socially acquainted with Dark Man, who went to Kingston University and had recently moved from the ends to Kingston, but was originally from Uganda. Dark Man got his name because of the colour of his skin. He was so black that in the right lighting he was almost a shade of purple. Not a known gang member, Dark Man was considered a nerd who was good at football and one of the only people in the clique with a mother who would let up to ten of us at a time hang out in her house. Her motto was: As long as we weren't out in the streets getting into trouble then her job in the community was done. It's almost surreal how naive and blind a parent can be towards their children's independent activities even when the signs are right there in their own homes.

Dark Man and I started to roll together and we got tight. He drifted from his books and football and joined the gang wars while I stayed trying to think of ways to make money. My ideas were put together with so much thought that it was almost impossible for Dark Man to back down. Even he, with all his book smarts, had to agree that my plans were sound. He would attend University during the week and play gangster on the weekends. I was used to the set up we had until one day he came back talking about,

"Que, brouv! I got a move, brouv."

"What you talking about?" I mocked him. Everyone in the hood knew I was the man for doing robberies.

"This one's easy," he boasted. "It's a two minute thing." I listened and his plan seemed to be on point. I was a specialist in the field and I knew he was trying to hype me up to get with it.

"Look, man's got a driver, a place for us to cotch (Chill out) after the thing." he said to convince me. I was making money selling drugs in Camden. Cocaine and heroin fetched a fair amount in the city. Wealthy business men had caught the addiction, allowing young drug dealers like me to line our pockets nicely. I thought as he spoke, *I got a good thing here. There ain't no need for me to start robbing again. Besides, jumping on a movement with an outsider wasn't advisable.* Dark Man and I hadn't got down like that before and most importantly I didn't want to go to jail. I listened to Dark Man run down his plan and instantly confirmed my co-operation in the mission when I received seven thousand pounds as an upfront instalment.

"I knew you'd be with it, Que. Dats why I hollered"

"Say no more, init." I was excited, I had seven grand burning a hole in my pocket.

"Twelve o'clock yeah?"

"Yeah." I nodded when we parted after arranging to meet the following Friday when the robbery was to go down.

18th October 2002 11:19AM

Some things in life you never forget and the heat from that afternoon would always be in my memory. It was Friday and I'd made plans to visit my Dad. It wasn't like him to be at home on a Friday; he was usually occupied with work. We decided to visit my Gran since she had stressed to my dad a number of times that she hadn't appreciated our absence on her birthday two weeks before.

"You ave fi no how fi read da ladies Gwent. She carn be mad if we go see 'er together. Ah long time since she see us both", my dad shouted to me from his room.

"Yeah I know", I muttered as I sat on my bed in a room I hadn't seen for almost two years. I thought about all the memories I had in this house, both good times and bad, but before I got too deep my phone rang. It was Dark Man. Watching his name flash on my screen, I knew what he wanted. It was time. I thought about going to my Gran's with my dad, but the thought of robbing someone gave me such a high I knew I wouldn't come down from until I was in and out. What's theirs was mine.

"Dad! What time you looking to go to Gran's? You looking to go soon?" I called upstairs, tired of stalling for time.

"Nah, a lickle (little) bit later down," he replied. So I bounced. I looked at my phone and Dark Man's name flashed again.

"Yo, I'm outside, brouv. Come on, man." he said as soon as I answered.

"I'm coming, where you?"

"I'm outside, c'mon." He ended the call, leaving me just about enough time to say bye to my dad and grab my hoodie. As usual I knew my father was disappointed that I wasn't going to spend the day with him as planned. But I didn't expect him to understand.

Dark Man sat outside my block in a small silver Mitsubishi Colt, but he wasn't in the driver's seat. That's strange, I thought. When he ran the plan down the week before we spoke about the car but I assumed he was going to be driving it.

"Get in, Que," Dark Man hollered as I got closer to his choice of transportation. What the fuck? Nah I couldn't believe it. A strange nerdy-looking African boy with a tough round face occupied the driver's seat while a hard-faced African girl sat in the back.

"Slide in there next to Ola-Femi." Dark Man got out the car with a smile on his face, opened his side of the car, and pulled back his seat for me to get in. Silently, I clenched my teeth and got in. I was pissed with Dark Man. There was a golden rule in the hood and he'd broken it Never let a man you don't know see where you lay your head. Dark Man was new to the roads. It was my fault I should have let him know, but its common sense. I kept quiet, never said a word until we got to Forest Gate. The African driver stopped the car, pulled back his seat and let "Ougly" next to me get out before slamming the door shut and passionately kissing her on the lips. I felt sick watching those two ugly Africans kissing. I checked out my surroundings and knew exactly where we were.

"Que, dis is Orbery." Dark Man said, finally formally introducing me to the driver.

"What's up, friend?"

"You cool." We clocked eyes in the rear view mirror and I nodded.

"Okay, we gonna be picking up my friend from university, Fem. He's gonna be setting up the guys that we gonna rob and then it's over to us, feel me," Dark man explained, causing confusion of my version of his initial plan.

"Run me through this," I said sternly. I weren't feeling the least bit comfortable sitting in a car with strangers, let alone making a move with them. It's too late for all dat now, Que, I told

106

myself deep in thought. Dark man directed the driver through South London, leading the way through clear narrow country roads. For about ten minutes there was nothing but fields and sky. On the side of the pavement I then saw another dark-skinned African boy with big eyes smiling at us. Instantly, I was put off. *Why is this boy smiling? We're about to do a move and this youth is smiling.* I just wanted to do what I came to do and get off at the nearest stop; I stayed because I was there now. It was too late to back out of this unprofessional move.

Five minutes around the corner and the driver killed the engine and exited the car. I watched him through my window as he disappeared around a building. *I knew this part of the plan,* I thought. *He's gonna get the van, the van we need to load our stolen goods into.* Dark Man's plan was for us to rob a couple of men who drove the distribution Lorries for the Evisu factory. Evisu was all in the streets in 2001 it was the "affordable designer label" that gave everybody in the hood a chance to shine. A pair of jeans could easily go for two hundred pounds which seemed to make the lick worth the ride.

Stupid Motherfuckers, I thought to myself as I watched the first two Lorries pull out. I wasn't worried about them calling the police. Those crooked ass workers were supposed to drive from the factory to the stores. Instead, they were stealing out of their own trucks and selling clothes to hustlers, trying to make a little cash on the side. I knew what I had to do and I was ready.

"Get the fuck out now!" I shouted, jumping out the car, but nice and calm. At the same time I was scanning my surroundings in case there were cameras or people looking. I walked up to the lorry, pulling open the door and grabbing one of the passengers out and onto the ground.

"Don't fucking move! Don't you fucking move!" I said to the driver, stealing a second to look back at Dark Man and Fem. who had panicked all they had to do was take the men's phones I looked at their stunned faces and cringed.

"Empty the truck!" I shouted frantically. They started

unloading the merchandise onto the ground and before long the pavement was covered. Seven minutes had gone by and still no sign of this van and Orbery, the driver.

"Shit, we're going jail! Shit! Shit! Shit!" I became frustrated because we had a rule: If you're still at the scene of the crime after five minutes you were going to prison.

"Where the fuck's your boy? We're going to jail. You know dat, right?" I shouted over to Dark Man, who moved slyly to the side of the road to make his call.

"Yo, brouv, where are you? What do you mean brouv? We're waiting on you to come through with the van." He continued on the phone telling the driver what street we were on and to come quick.

Nah this is doggie, I thought. *Why you telling him what street we're on? He knows dat already.* I looked at Dark Man and his friend looking through the stolen goods on the ground. Something told me to go. I made a decision to jump in the truck and drive it around the corner. I didn't want any part of what was about to go down but I was in over my head.

I couldn't believe what I saw when I walked back. Dark Man and Fem were loading the same car we came in a panic. I can't believe this shit! I thought. But there was no time to ask questions. I'd deal with Dark Man when we were safe.

"Hurry up!" we shouted back and forth, trying to stuff every item of clothing into any vacant space left in the car.

"Blood, get the fuck out!" I stopped to wipe my brow and noticed the driver sitting comfortably in his seat looking like we were putting him out. Like he had somewhere else to be. "I said get the fuck out and pack this shit up before I blow your brains all over this car!" We were well into ten minutes at the scene. Orbery got out and started packing the car. By now it was jammed pack and we we're just getting ready to slam the boot shut.

"Ahh shit! The fucking police!" I saw the first car coming up behind us and I knew there was no time to jump in the car. There's no way I'm going jail for this without trying to at least get away.

The only option left was to run. Dark Man and the driver went one way and me and his friend, Fem, with the big eyes ran in the other direction and straight into the police. The chase was on. We picked up speed and three uniformed officers chased us in hopes of us slipping up and being caught. I didn't know where I was running, but I knew I had to get away so I ran down a side road and jumped over a fence, landing in sewage I ran along the sewer holding my breath from the stench then climbed over a wall fenced with barb wire cutting deep gashes in both my hands.

Grunting at the pain while still running, blood poured from my flesh wounds and I could hear police dogs barking, which made me even more determined to get away. I hid in the bushes in the sewage for over an hour until I couldn't hear any more police sirens. Looking at the wall in front of me with the barb wire on the top, I knew that was my route to freedom. With my hands already numb from the previous injuries, I climbed the wall with much strength and felt nothing but relief. I looked like a tramp in designer clothing. I checked my surroundings and spotted a train station.

"All stops to Mary Land!" the conductor called before the last passengers huddled toward the doors to board. I jumped on behind a man and his bike and changed trains until I was far away from the scene of the crime. In the end I ended up at London Bridge station, so I got a 149 bus which took me back to the block.

"Who's that?" my dad called down stairs, hearing the front door open and close.

"It's me, dad," I said, quickly making my way to my room and shutting the door. That night I burned the clothes I wore during the robbery, showered, and continually tried to get into contact with Dark Man with much fail. By the following day I was desperate to know the status of the situation and went to visit Dark Man at home.

"What's up, Que?" Dark Man's little brother opened the door just wide enough for me to peek through.

"You cool, Lil' Man where's your brother?" I asked the young boy.

"Ain't you man heard? He got shifted yesterday?" I listened to him tell me what went down with Dark Man, Fem, and the drive. They were arrested and detained pending a court case. I was the only one who got away.

CHAPTER THIRTEEN |

"**I**'m so tired of his bullshit Carlton; I don't want those people banging down my door anymore. You tell Gwenton to sort his shit out before I sort it out for him!" Joyce said to my dad sound as if she had been crying.

"Calm nah woman, ah talk. Let mi talk to 'im. Ello."

"Dad!"

"Gwenton let me ask you something."

Oh shit! I thought to myself. When my father called me I could hear him and Joyce cursing each other before he'd addressed me on the phone.

"Sure, Dad." I couldn't think of what I'd done that would

have him on my case.

"Ah wah you do mek di police ah bang down Joyce door? And don't lie to me, Gwenton" Growing up my father often asked questions in which he didn't care for the answer. He'd brought me up to distinguish the difference between wrong and right and I knew he wanted me to put what I'd done wrong, right.

I listened to him speak and it turned out that Orbery Dark Man's driver having picked me up from my dad's house on the day of the robbery had shown the police where I lived. They had come looking for me. This was the very reason I was pissed at Dark Man on the day of the move, but lucky for me I didn't live at my dad's, I wasn't worried about the constant threats the police were making to knock off my step-mums door if I didn't turn myself in. for a month I stayed away from the block until guilt started to set in. I realized it wasn't fair for the police to keep hassling my dad and step-mum. And them having to live with the embarrassment of the neighbours seeing the police parked up every day trying to capture me with no luck.

***

I was detained for six long months while the prosecution gathered their armed robbery charges. They ain't got shit on me, I kept telling myself from the start. I applied for bail, but they turned me down. Reason being that they had found a gun wrapped in a sock and felt it was the gun used in the robbery. They were afraid if I got bail I might intimidate the victim and the driver, who had now been placed in police protection. The police were now going to use him against us as to testify in court.

"If this guy turns up in court, we're done." I told Dark Man when I got the chance.

"Brouv, I swear, man ain't gonna turn up. He ain't gonna shit on us," Dark Man reassured me, but inside I didn't trust his word. Orbery had told the police where I lived. He didn't give a fuck about me. I awaited my first day in court.

Here goes, I said as I paced into the court. With my hands

cuffed I was presented in front of the judge and jury as Gwenton Sloley, well known gang member and thug who resided in the London borough of Hackney. The distasteful look on the judge's face was clear: Guilty! We caught each other's eyes then he was interrupted by a policeman's announcement.

"The witness in question, Orbery has been presumed missing at this moment of time and will not be present this afternoon," he said.

I can't believe it. There's no way we can get done for this. He ain't here to give evidence. We're going home. I was elated. The trial continued and all the other witnesses gave a different account of what they had both seen and heard *Okay this is looking good.* My spirits were high during the break, but during the second session the pressure started to kick in. The jury couldn't make up their mind whether we we're guilty based on the accounts presented to them.

"The prosecution calls for a break," a member of the court called out. I was confused looking around I watched the jury leave the court room and waited with my freedom in their hands.

"All rise!" This is it. I breathed out slowly, I might go to jail. I'd already been detained for six months and that was just about all I could take. At this moment I was remorseful. With no evidence we were still found guilty on joint enterprise, which meant if they found one guilty we were all guilty.

No. I can't fucking believe this in happening to me. I'm only nineteen! My mind was doing overtime. During the prosecution's turn to present its case, it had come to light that the driver wasn't snitching on us, but really didn't know about the robbery. He was only tricked into it at the last minute by Dark Man. I knew I was going to be in prison for another two and half years. If I got parole I would have to do an extra year. I got in contact with Trav. I was already looking at doing four years for robbery and thought I could get the charges for the stabbing he was being held for to run concurrent. I told Trav to blame it all on me and I'd take the rap as I was already in prison, but he refused to listen. His like that. Once his minds is made up that's it. Luckily, he got off the case and was given a second chance.

I told Charleen that I thought it would be better for her to find someone else, but she refused and assured me she could wait another three and half years.

"Que, I don't want no body but you," she had said. Eventually, she did exactly what I thought she would and cheated on me with another drug dealer.

I went through the court process and was tried as an adult. Automatically, I was transferred to a different prison for young offenders called Portland YOI (young offenders institute) When I turned of age, I got moved to the county prison called Swinfen Hall in Lichfield, a long way from London. It was occupied by inmates referred to as "The Big Boys." I entered Swinfen Hall, a child amongst grown men seventy-five percent of the inmates were from Birmingham and had a natural hatred for Londoners. Welcomed by dirty looks and threats had me deciding to form a gang with the people I came up with on the prison bus. They were feeling the same, but needed a front man to set the pace. I guess that was me and I was up for the job. My twentieth birthday came and went and I spent the rest of the year building up a gang made up of all prisoners from London. I wasn't gonna let no country boys take me for a mug. A couple inmates respected that and joined up. Soon after, a lot more inmates came out of the wood-works, admitting that they weren't from Birmingham or Nottingham. They'd just said that because they were too afraid to say they were from London.

"Brouv, man couldn't say we was from London before man come here,. We're out numbered in here. What's to stop us from being attacked? It's like for every one of us there's twenty of them." an inmate once confided in me. Most of the people I teamed up with were from South London, but respected my gangster. Going into Swinfen taught me who I really was and how far I would go when my back was against the wall. But compared to the roads, admittedly it was the first time I'd really ever had to stand my ground and prove myself.

I spent most of my time in Swinfen Hall causing trouble to the point where the prison guards made a deal with me: If I calmed down the London boys I'd be allowed to be transferred to a London jail taking the next bus out. I was happy with that deal. It was too far for my family to keep coming to visit me. I was only there for a year of my sentence so I didn't take part in any of their courses. My mind was on survival.

I calmed down all the London boy's on my team within a couple of week, and nothing. The system lied. With my permission the Londoners took over the prison and by the end of the month the officers had made a wise decision to transfer me to keep the peace.

"Sloley, get up and get your things together."It was just after five in the morning when an officer opened my cell and told me to gather my belongings. I thought I was dreaming. Yes, I'm getting out of here. As quickly as I could, I sprang to my feet and started clearing the small shelf welded into the wall above my bed. Toothpaste, tooth brush, cocoa butter, deodorant. I was startled by the presence of another officer in my cell.

"Come on, Sloley, they're waiting for you," he said. I was cuffed and led with an officer both in front and behind me onto the wing and out through the entrance of the prison. Containment had filled me with mixed emotions. I was blinded by the capacity of space surrounding me and deafened by the sound of my heart racing. I was nauseous.

"Single file," the officer said, loading myself and a few other inmates into a large prison van that had 1x1 compartments just small enough for one prisoner to be contained in.

"Stop here." I was told. Taken to my compartment, I was handed a plastic cup full of water and locked in.

"Oi, where you taking me? I fucking hate you pigs!" an inmate four compartments down began banging his wall. It was uncomfortable sitting in such a tight space with a single tinted window as our only source of light.

"I can't breathe!-I can't fucking breathe!" he shouted.

"Clark, just calm down and shut up," I heard the officer say but Clark continued to kick his door.

It must have been a quarter past six when we pulled off. I remember looking out the window and watching early morning travellers already on their way to work. It was wet outside, and I listened to the wheels of the prison van drive through puddles and splash the curb until eventually I dozed off.

During my three year sentence I had been transferred in and out of nine different prisons. I spent my first months in HMP (Her Majesty's Pleasure) High Down and HMP Portland and the rest were spent between HMP Coldingley, HMP Bullingdon, HMP Aylesbury, HMP Pentonville, HMP Belmarsh, until I was released in November 2005 from HMP High Point. I seemed to have the same problem everywhere I went, gang affiliation. I had that leader's glow deemed a born leader. I found the ability to captivate an audience and hold their attention. During this time I found that I had the gift of influence.

I spent six weeks in HMP Belmarsh locked up for 23 hours a day with all the so- called hard nuts from different local boroughs all trying to be top dog. I had already completed two years of my sentence and had met a lot of people there, who like me, had been transferred there. I was friends with people from all over London, people I'd met both in prison and out. I'd spent a lot of my social time in the yard and yet still, I had to deal with the pressures of the streets under surveillance.

I remember this one day me, Redz, Short Man and DC, some of the guys I rolled with at the time, were on the yard. I could see some Tottenham boys pretending to plan an attack on an older Hackney boy. He was in there on a murder charge for killing a well known Tottenham boy, who was one of the leaders of the TMD boys.

"Que, you better move to my guy, 'cause his is going to get shanked," one of the Tottenham boys came up to me and said. I laughed.

"No one ain't moving to him 'cause when we was on the wing you lot didn't want to do any-thing. If a man killed one of my boys I'd cut him on sight. You lot are all actors." The Hackney boy was an older Fields boy, so I could have left him to die, but I respected him for being the only real Hackney guys when it came to taking out a Tottenham boy., Word had got around about my little discussion and at last, Mr. Older Fields guy respected me. I felt like I had the power because if the Tottenham boys decided to go ahead with the plan, I would have jumped in. Then all hell would have broken out in the prison. Or, I could have let the older get stabbed or possibly killed because he was out numbered 10 to 1. I knew the other Hackney boys on the yard were soft and would have run when it kicked off.

CHAPTER: FOURTEEN |-

Watching my dad shift in his seat in front of me, and seeing the pain and disappointment in his eyes tore my heart apart. I was ashamed. Knowing he knew of the double life I led and having to endure his lectures on how he'd brought me up to know better was almost worst than a four year sentence.

"I'm cool, Dad," I said, sitting in front of him in my inmate attire. I was a child ashamed. Not a day went by while I was incarcerated that I didn't regret not listening to him. I had caused him so much heartache and pain, yet he continued to love and support me in his own way. He was now all I had, the only other blood-line I had on this earth. My mum's family would not have come to find me if she wasn't on her death bed and my dad's side of family would have left me in Jamaica if he hadn't brought me to England.

Growing up, I found out that before my arrival my dad fell out with his sisters because they told my gran not to agree to sign for me to come to England. They thought my dad would dump me on my gran, even though she was well into her 60s, past looking after children. Dad's visits brought no pleasure, just reminders of the life I'd left behind. I craved the streets and now resided in a place where there was nowhere to call home. I imagined the world moving on without me like in the movies when a gang member goes to jail and gets out a decade later and everybody and everything he left behind had changed, evolved even Try as I may, I watched my back and only really spoke when I was being spoken directly to. In time I came to find that being new in a jail is like being a learner driver Your anxiety makes you stick out like a was an unstable soul. Inmates had good days and bad days and everyday was an experience.

If I don't get out of here I'm gonna go mad, I vented, slamming down the phone and returning to my cell. I was almost at the breaking point living a double life, the life of a leader with prison number JC6233, a number I will remember for the rest of my life.

Loose lips sinks ships, I remembered Coolie Lee saying to me that afternoon after school. I was mad with Dark Man for setting me up, mad at the system I was incarcerated in, but mostly I was mad at my boys back home.

I wish I was dead. This wasn't the first time I'd felt like dying, falsifying freedom with death. There were countless number of young men just like me exploiting their freedom out on the streets. Because of me, boys I'd made my soldiers (those whom I'd looked after from school) stuck by when nobody else would and allowed them to bask in my hood success. I sat on the edge of my bed and slammed my fist on my desk while thinking about the nerve of some of these same boys sending me death threats. One man's failure is another man's success. With one less mouth to feed and a vacant position for a general, everybody wanted to be top man. Prison had me restrained. I wanted to maintain my position on the streets, but I was in no position to demand respect. That was something I would have to deal with when I got home. In here, there were no empty threats. Real gangsters walked the yard and at a snap of a finger could find justification for brutally attacking you. Stabbing you with a self adhered sharp object or even causing your death. Taking a life is nothing to a man already incarcerated for life.

120

This place is his domain and every now and then he will do something to make sure all the other inmates are aware of his position.

"Watch, brouv, you think man's joking. I'm gonna fuck you up," a baby faced inmate shouted through the cell late one night. "Watch till the morning, init," he continued, making threats to a guy in a cell about seven doors down from his.

"I beg you, shut the fuck up and go to sleep. Men out 'ere are trying to sleep," another inmate roared dreading the annoying inmates banter and all the other chatter on the wing.

In the morning I heard the metal sliding in the cell doors leading up to mine, but remained seated on my bed. I never ran to my cell door when the officers opened them. I was in no rush to get out only to be locked back up.

"What's good, Que?" a white boy two cells down from me asked as I made my way to the dining hall.

I nodded as I passed inmates on the wing. I know there's gonna be something popping off in here today after what went down last night, I thought just seconds before it happened.

"Ahhhhhh, my face!!" I only saw what happened because it happened so fast. Life in prison moves slow. You don't run because you're never in a rush, but this dude caught my attention. No sooner than two minutes after the officer had opened the cells and released the prisoners onto the wing, had the submissive inmate, armed with a plastic cup filled with a mixture of piping hot sugar water. Like many other inmates, I couldn't help but cover my ears. The boy screamed out like a restrained cat then wailed profoundly like a new-born baby, instantly touching his face uncertain of the damage he'd sustained. I hated seeing people in excruciating pain, but I couldn't look away. It's like I had to see because I never knew if the next time it would be me.

"Help me!" he screamed out to the officers, his face peeling off in his hands, leaving the reddish-white tissue on show.

This is where society had placed me, not against my own will, but because I wanted to prove that "I'm down. I'm bad I am a gangster." What was I thinking? Never in my wildest dreams had I imagined my life to be like this. Although I was warned of the consequences of my actions, I never thought this would be happening to me.

CHAPTER: FIFTEEN |-

Two years had passed since my last breath of air as a free man. I was nineteen at the time of conviction, confused at who I was and not knowing the consequences of what I wanted to be at twenty-one and still young. I had travelled a long heartbreaking road and currently resided in Bullingdon Prison, Category B one down from an A Category maximum security prison, Bullingdon was the worst of the worst. The inmates consisted of "bent officers," officers who were ready to bring anything in the prison for a little extra money pretend rude boys who were nobody outside prison and people who took pride in the crimes they'd committed. Bullingdon gave me time to reflect on my life before jail. I came to the conclusion that what led me down this road was my poor choice of friends. Your peers are the biggest influences on the streets and they came with many good attributes as well as down falls Before I came to jail I belonged to a gang and had more friends and associates than I could count, boys who said they would die for me. Men, I'd sat in cars next to while they'd bust their guns People I'd lent money to. I spent so much time trying to prove I was *real* when the lifestyle and the people in it were *fake*. During my thirty-six month sentence I realized I would never be out partying, taking advantage of the sun setting above me or even having the pleasure of smelling a fresh pot of rice and peas being cooked on a Sunday morning.

My last year of incarceration I kept my head down. I was moved once more to HMP High Point where I was to spend the remainder of my sentence until I would be released in November I spoke to very little people from my past and having visitors was deemed almost impossible, considering I had been situated outside of London Towards the end of my sentence I felt stronger than ever. I believed in myself and thought I had the ability to go right where I was going wrong.

Word on the streets was that there was a new set of LOMs. Younger's and the Olders were taxing drug dealers from outside the borough, setting up a system that enabled them to completely take over Hoxton. Allowing the younger's a place to make money and keeping the constant flow of crack for cash fluent. Things seemed to be going well for them, and some members had even gone as far as inking their set on their body, tattooing their hands, necks, and arms. Even the Olders that were still in the area trying to beat their drug addictions and stay out of prison were getting inked up. I couldn't understand the sense behind that. Yeah, they were repping their set, but gang affiliation was illegal and they were labelling themselves gang members for life. Looking back at the scene now, I could see how the Olders engaged the Younger's and used them as inspiration to keeping their thirty and forty something year old lives thriving in the streets. It was all about reputation. Even some of the new members we tried to take out before I went to prison, known as gang hoppers, always wanted to be with the strongest team of the season, were now members of LOM.

CHAPTER: SIXTEEN |

Thursday November 17 2005: 7:00 P.M.

With my skin glistening in the dim lighting on the wing and the fresh sent of soap still on my presence I stood against the fence leading to the yard and scanned the area for my usual ring of inmate chums.

"What's good, fam'?" My right hand man, Eric approached me with a pound and a standard hood style hug. "Where you been, bruv?" he asked, leaning up against the fencing beside me.

"Showers," I simple answered and followed suit as Eric then made his way back to the table he was seated at before my arrival.

"What's good?" I acknowledged the rest of my peers before slumming into a seat in the corner.

I guess my spirit wanted out of this cage, but my mind was happy to stay. Less than thirty minutes ago I was hitting the showers, oblivious to the discharge sheet that awaited me in my cell. Now here I was with less than twenty-four hours before my release engaged in idle chit-chat, content with my company and surroundings.

"Man, I'm telling you, I'm getting tired of waiting on this

125

damn release sheet." Eric spoke above the murmurs within the group hurdled around the small table, snapping me out of my thoughts.

"What'd you say?" I lifted my head and asked.

"These screws don't respect us, man, cos we black I'm telling you," he continued in his broken English accent, shaking his head all the while. It was like preaching when Eric and I broke out in conversation. The surrounding group nodded in agreement, feeding his ego with complaints of their own.

"For real doh'. How long you been here now?" Obtaining my full attention, Eric was adamant to get me to join his pity party. "I dunno." I shrugged, although I'd known exactly how long I'd been incarcerated, thirty-six months, three years to the date, to be exact. Without thinking I rose from my seat and made my way to my cell, leaving Eric and the others to continue their idle chat, I was getting ready to pack. Tomorrow couldn't come sooner. Within twenty minutes I'd sold all my belongings, apart from a single bottle of cream and a roll-on. I'd have everything I needed on the outside, I told myself before my thoughts were interrupted by noise on the wing.

With my hands in my pockets, I strode from my bed to my door, leaned against the frame. I looked from the rowdy crowd of inmates socializing on either sides of the wing to the map of London on my TV as Eastenders began and made a choice. I wanted to go home and not a damn thing was going to stop me. *If those clowns want to cause a riot over some card game then they could do it on their own time.* Hidden behind the door in my very own combined space I allowed my mind to block out the prison ruckus and thought about my life as a free man. Robbing people in the street was easy, stealing cars, and selling drugs was primary school stuff for a man like me. I knew what I was doing. I was calling the shots. *Damn,* I thought, *I've been shot at, wrestled men two times my age, but none of that scared me more that the thought of becoming a legitimate member of my community.* Don't get me wrong, I wanted to change. This wasn't the life I wanted to own, but I didn't want my future to be a replay of gang members before me that had gone legitimate and fallen. In my cell alone just before the crews called for bang up, I thought of all the people I'd lost to the streets, *Monty*. And then I thought of my mother. Either way life ain't fair. I fought back tears. She devoted her life to the church and was an upstanding member of her community, sometimes working as many as four jobs at a time. *What was the point?* I retired to my bed, laying flat on top of the inch fin mattress. What was the point in adhering all these rules in society when either way you were gonna die?

Everybody gwan die, Gwenton, but it's how you die that matters. For the first time in my sentence I was grateful for my solitude. I pulled the sleeves of my blue coloured jumper over my fists and wiped my eyes. My mother died a hard working woman, who instead of joining a gang, found solitude in the church. She was respected and loved by people who considered her their sister. I wanted to make her proud, and not just her, but I wanted to find pride in myself. I tossed and turned that night, weighing the highs and the lows, the pros and the cons of giving up my street life and going it alone.

CHAPTER: SEVENTEEN |

Being escorted by two weighty officers through the large steel gates that separated me and my peers from incarceration and freedom, I felt a cold chill run down my spine. I was gonna be free. "Roll up!" an officer yelled through the slot in my cell door. It was a little after eight in the morning and I was wide awake, I had been for hours, thinking, *Am I really being released today? Nah, this is a joke. I'll just wait until they call me, then I can get my hopes up.*

"Come on, Sloley. Roll up or you planning on staying with us?" Backtracking officer Evans peered into my cell. I'd been here long enough to know what "Roll up" meant and I wasn't going to wait for him to tell me again. Quickly, I began gathering up my bedding, mattress, pillow and other belongings. You leave nothing for the next inmate. Nothing but bare walls, a drafty window, and lime scale on the toilet and sink. *Okay, this is really happening!* Familiar with the sound of the steel inside my cell door being unlatched, I exhaled and awaited orders.

"You know the drill, Sloley." *One last time.* I nodded, placing my hands together outwards to be cuffed before being escorted to the front office.

Dressed in my old street clothes, my jeans tight at the crotch, and my jacket two sizes too small, I anticipated my departure.

The deputy pushed a property release form in front of me to sign. I looked at the piece of paper and frowned. The form held a list of the property in your possession at the time of your conviction. Using my left hand, I wiped sweat off my brow and looked at both officers on either side of me. Before reaching for a pen I directed my attention to the items listed on the form. A set of keys to my step-mothers home in Stoke Newington, my old Nokia phone and my probation officer name and address and what time I would have to report there today. How long I would have to do on licence and I agree not committee any crimes while on licence. I was leaving with what I came with, *nothing.* But never the less, I was leaving. Positioning my hand ready to sign, all kinds of thoughts ran though my head. *What if they hold me? Threaten to keep me here if I refuse to sign?* I thought for a moment. *If they don't have authority to hold you, they don't have authority. They are hoping you'll make their job easy by voluntarily submitting. I knew first-hand that they couldn't keep you in jail forever. They have to let you go. Eventually, they run out of cause.* Yet, I knew the officers would do everything they can to get an inmate to cave in, to change your "Yes" to a "No." *Never the less*, I signed the form and all the other related paper work contracting me to parole. I would have to meet up and keep appointments with a parole officer for the remaining three years of my would be sentence.

I felt like Tim Robbins in that old school movie "Shaw shank Redemption" when he finally crawled out the gutter after his escape, except I was being released. I had served 36 months and 2 days incarcerated under her majesty's pleasure —-had endless dreams of my freedom, but as I stood on the other side of the steel gate escorted by both officers still at my side, I was dumb-founded. I'd grown accustomed to the rules of incarceration, being told when to wash, eat, and sleep. It had become a part of my normal routine. Sure, I wanted to get back to society and reclaim my place in my community. But I didn't know what awaited me on the other side of the gate, and I was reluctant to find out.

At 10:59 A.M. I was finally released into civilization.

"General, show me some love, brouv?"

"Shit!" was all I was able to muster. Greeks opened the passenger side door to Turk's MLK Mercedes and casually strode my way. We embraced in a brother like hug, both of us taking a moment of silence before Klinton hollered at me through the window.

"What's good, fam?-You're free! Come get in this car before they lock your black ass up again," he joked. Just meters away from my last place of residence I put some soul in my step and made my way to my ride. I was pleased that my people had come to collect me. I made a mental note of who had shown me love while I was locked down and Greeks had always remained at the top of my list.

"Welcome home, Gwenton," my step-mother greeted me. As I entered the car, we embraced.

"Rah, you bulked up, Que," Turk, who occupied the back seat with Klinton and my step-mum, commented on my stature. Physically, I had changed while mentally I was struggling to move on.

"Come on, man. Greek's, get me out of 'ere." I need say no more. Greeks' car screeched as he drove out of the court-yard of the prison. I couldn't wait to get ghost from the building. My nerves were unsettled and I began fidgeting in my seat. I had committed so many crimes and offences that I needed to be far away from the building to really come to grips with my release. I had committed countless numbers of offences while I was on the road, I didn't want to take the chance of hanging around and being banged up for another something years.

"Where you wanna go, Que?"

"What you think? I'm starving out 'ere. I wanna eat. Fuck that, I wanna munch."

"Mackey Dee's?"

"Yeah whatever," I said, adjusting my seat. Greek's filled the sometimes awkward silence with the sound of the radio and it wasn't long before I found myself bopping my head to the rhyme a young up and coming rapper was spitting on a hot beat.

Bringing the car to a stop, Greeks turned the radio off and parked. The five of us got out the car, clowning. It felt like Christmas without the wrapped gifts. We made and entrance in the diner, talking loud and getting in each other's space.

"Look at you all big and shit."

"Fuck you, Turk, move." Playfully pushing past Turk I rolled into Mc-Donald's carrying the hunger of about twenty slaves.

"Hi, can I take your order? Sir, are you being served?" the weave wearing woman behind the counter asked me as I approached.

"Umm, Nah. I'll have a large hamburger meal with extra fries." I looked her over and answered. She was staring at me it had been years since a woman had looked at me the way she was do.

"And what drink?" She licked her lips

"Still Fanta.-Nah, I mean give me a milkshake, banana!" I smiled to myself thinking of something more appetizing than food.

"Here, brouv." I could have laughed when Greek's pulled out a wad of folded notes, peeling off a tenner to pay for my food.

"Nah, I got this." I pulled out a smaller wad of cash. I was given eighty pounds on my release and also the four hundred pounds I'd saved on my canteen balance. I wanted to make a bit of change coming up to my release. One of the first lessons I'd learnt in life is that if you always rely on people, eventually they will let you down.

"Mum, lend me a fiver so I can get something to eat?" I heard Klinton ask my step-mum, even thought he thought he'd lowered his voice so no one would hear. *I guess some things never change.* Here we were three years later and Klinton was still asking his mum for money. I shook my head. Klinton wasn't the only person who hadn't changed since I'd been away. When we drove into Stoke Newington Estate, the whole block still looked the same.

"What's good, Que?" Roderick come around my parts to show me love.

"Rah, I ain't seen you in a hot minute." After three years I was still the man on the block.

"I heard you been inside. You good, doh?"

"Yeah, I'm cool," I told Super, one of the older boys on the block. As I made my way up the stairs in the flat, he gave me his number then we went our separate ways. He continued up the stairs and I stopped on the ground floor. I imagined my step-mum's house to be filled with all the latest and most modern technology, flat screen televisions like on the Curry's adverts. There was new carpet and a fresh lick of paint. Reluctantly, I waited for my dad to come home. He'd told me he'd put away a couple hundred pounds for me while I was gone, but like I thought, all the stories and promises about me being okay for money were just jail talk. People have a lot to say when you're locked up. Girls with the "I've always loved you" and "I'm gonna be faithful and wait for you" was expected, but I was half hoping that my father would come through for me. Not just to line my pockets, but to give me another option.

"Yo, Que, you jamming or you coming down?" Greeks poked his head around my door. I thought of the wad of money Greeks had in his pocket compared to mine and sighed. When my father returned, he handed me a twenty pound note and a half-hearted hug. I wasn't ungrateful; I was scared and back at square one, broke.

Turk and Greeks took me to Wood Green Shopping Centre, which earned them much love from me. Especially seeing as Greeks himself had only just been released a few months prior to me. They bought me a phone, a new black two-in--one Nike jacket, and a few other everyday items of clothing to get me on my feet. Seeing them both peel off a note irritated me in the worst way. I had no money of my own. I'd planned on going straight, but my gut feeling was to jump on any movement, anything to put money in my pocket and place me back on top.

"Turk, let me holler at you for a minute." I motioned him to exit the car with me as the three of us decided to call it a day.

"What's good?"

"I need to hold 400 pounds from you." I just put it out there straight .Turk knew I wasn't into playing games and he'd been around long enough to know of my reputation on the streets.

"I need to get back up, you know?"

"I hear dat, brouv." He nodded his head like it was a shame to see me broke. "When you wanna get dat?"

"Let me get back to you, but I'm gonna be needing it ASAP."

"I got you," he said, getting back in the car leaving me alone on the block. I was thinking, *With the four hundred I saved from prison and his four hundred I can buy an ounce of crack cocaine and personally supply the older dudes in the area that were still smoking the stuff. Now, I can't go buy it myself. Nah that would be stupid.* I'd call Super because he was well known by the older guys. You could even go as far as saying he was "The Man" when I was growing up. He had all the girls, fast cars, and was almost famous for being "Just Super." He used to cut my hair as a kid. In fact, he was just another known face in the hood. His extravagant lifestyle proved too much for him and he later suffered a break-down where he was admitted to Homerton hospital's mental ward. Super really was a cool guy. After he got knocked off his throne, it seemed as if I was the only one out of all his friends and girls to visit him in his time of need. I took him cigarettes to smoke weekly until he was back to normal, and was resettled in his own flat.

I couldn't have been a bigger fool than I had been in prison for three years. The first thing I did was hand over eight hundred pounds, no questions asked. I knew nothing about what had been happening on the streets. Had I been filled in, I would have known that Super was no longer respected in these parts. Just five minutes after I'd dropped him to his suppliers house did he come running back around the corner saying, "Que, I been robbed!" I was so mad I laughed.

"Just get in the car. Don't worry about it. It's only eight hundred pounds." I mumbled the last bit, because who was I kidding? I had nothing else to get me on my feet. I was pissed. I told Klinton and Turk about what happened and their instant reaction was to get violent.

"Aye, aye!" I tried to calm them down. "It's cool, let's just forget it and move on." I was so vexed that keeping quite was the only way I could stop myself from hurting someone.

CHAPTER: EIGHTEEN |

Two weeks after my release I had begun robbing people again.-The first two drug dealers I robbed gave me my wheels. I brought myself a blue and white Yamaha R6 super bike and used it as my means of transport. Prior to my parole I was on a six months driving ban, but I was like, "The police can't catch me on a bike." I was almost back to my old ways, committing minor crimes, and hanging with the usual suspects. Inside I was battling the streets trying to get out, but wanting to leave with something. Reluctantly, I signed up for a counselling course at Hackney Community College. I had been carrying such heavy burdens throughout the years that I felt a need to connect and bring some kind of freedom and ending the suffering that young members of the community like me have endured.

"Gwenton, I just want to say that I'm sorry about what I did too."

"What you talking about?" I looked at my sister's features as she spoke to me and seeing so much of my mother in her.

"What I did to you when we were younger. I didn't mean to

do those things." *Oh God, please. I don't want to hear this,* was all I couldn't help thinking. But a part of me was desperate to know after all these years if my sister had really done the things my young mind had accused her of years ago in Jamaica. Faye had admitted she needed help getting over the things that we'd experienced in Jamaica and referred herself to receive counselling. I guess she thought that by telling another person about things that happened to her as a child would somehow make them go away. But it didn't. It didn't even help make things better.

Why did you do those things to me? I wanted to scream, but I had blocked those thoughts out for so many years that my denial had caused me to forget.

"It happened to me, Gwenton. When mum was out and you were playing in the back, your dad used to touch me. He raped me just like our grandfather raped our mum. I thought it was normal, so I did to you what was done to me. I didn't know it was wrong." I hated that I couldn't hate my sister for what she'd done to me. I'd have to live with this disgusting feeling for the rest of my life. I didn't ask for this. Maybe this is why while growing up I wasn't good with relationship. I'd always thought women wanted to use me for sex. I found it hard to love people because I never felt that love from my family.

Your dad used to touch me. Kept ringing in my head. I would never be able to bring myself to confront my father about the accusations Faye was making against him. I was just coming to terms with the sexual abuse my mother was subjected to by her father and I wasn't ready to open up another can of worms.

Emotionally, I detached myself from the first sight of love and called it lust, confused by the two. I kept many female friends, but committed to few relationships. Being sexually assaulted by a family member isn't something you can be open about in the lifestyle I lived, but my heart wanted to release this burden. I wanted to tell someone, "It happened to me. I struggled with it, rebelled against society and all its rules, but I'm still here!" Also, I wanted a better life, a life where I could walk on the streets without looking over my shoulder. The funny thing is, the more I stepped away from my peers and the gang life, the more I had to watch my back.

Back on the block, Klinton was back with his old friends and back to his old ways. Taking drugs and wilding out, except now he was the boss, ruling the estate with a firm hand. Being labelled as the top robber man of the area, he was feared and he meant business. Today, I still don't know if it was the drugs that sent him on his gangster road or if it was just him rebelling. Maybe he was trying to prove a point to me by making his own name on the street. People always knew him as Que's brother, even though he's the older brother. They were still talking the same mess they were talking before I was sentenced. They'd been plotting and planning the "move" that was gonna get them out the hood for as long as I could remember. Yet, the only moves he'd made were house robberies and stick up's. Still intoxicating himself with crack filled roll-ups, Klinton was robbing a different person every day with no regards to their status, connection, or even location. He was hitting people on our own block. Out to make money any which way he could, Klinton and his team would snatch a grown man from the bus stop if he had something pleasing to the eye. I had to give it to him and his team though, they moved like professionals. Klinton's team consisted of a few white boys in their late twenties, who would often dress up as police officers and huge henchmen. They bulked up in the gym daily, each of them meaning business. They rarely left the house and returned empty handed. Unfortunately for my step-mother this meant we had all kinds of illegal things in the house, be it small electrical, or large amounts of drugs and weapons.

Time rolled by without any warning and I was now seven months into my freedom. I was visiting my parole officer once a week as required. Since the police hadn't come knocking, I took that as a sign that my behaviour so far had been acceptable and I started to get comfortable with my new routine. See, I had an excuse before my step-mum would be hollering at both me and

Klinton to get a job or do something constructive with our time.

"You boys have had the same opportunities as everybody else." I'd listen, promise I'd get on it then tip-toe around her in the house, hoping she wouldn't question me about career choices or ask how my job search was going.

"What's the point?" I'd now answer back. "It's not like people's gonna wanna employ someone fresh out of jail, besides I'm still on parole." It worked all the time. She left the house for work and I nestled back into my bed. Eventually, she stopped with the questions and let me and Klinton be.

***

What the fuck! I quickly jumped out my sleep and sat upright in my bed after hearing a loud and disturbing thud. I knew it had to be after six in the morning because my dad left for work at six and I'd stirred in my sleep as he unlatched the door to leave. My freezer box room had its advantages being that it was so close to the front door.

I can't believe this is happening. I froze. *This has to be a dream. Am I dead? Or worst. The police. It was just a matter of time before they made a move at Klinton,* I thought, before my assumptions became clear.

"Its armed police, stay where you are. Don't move!" I obeyed and quickly turned over, laying face down in the bed with my arms and legs far apart. I was used to the prison crews tying to run up on me late at night to take my mobile phone.

Is this a joke? I wanted to laugh. A handful of more police officers came bursting through my door unarmed hesitant of their positions. Already in a restrain able position, I was taken into the hall where I saw Klinton being lead down the stairs. Half asleep he rubbed his eyes, probably thinking that same dream shit I was thinking when I was startled.

"Right names?" the bulky one that looked as if he was running the show asked.

"Klinton Davies"

"And?" Cutting my eyes, I answered, "Gwenton Sloley."

"Gwenton Sloley, huh?" I watched the officer spit out my

name like it was dirt and call something into his radio.

"Cuff him, cuff them both." Quickly, and without a fight the officers hand cuff me then my brother. I knew from the attitude they had when they were talking to me that they had already read my file. I couldn't help thinking; *I'm the good one now. My brother is the G, not me.* I wasn't worried because I knew they wouldn't find anything as I always tided my brother's mess before I went to bed. It's like I knew they were coming today. I could see them tearing up the house and getting upset because they couldn't find anything incriminating to support the information their informant had provided. By now we were both well aware of why the police had kicked off our door at half past six in the morning. A couple weeks back, Klinton had come up lucky and broke into a Turkish drug dealer's house. He broke into the owner's safe bearing enough fire-arms to start a war. Bringing all he could back with him, Klinton and his team decided to sell what they'd stolen. They brought in more money than I'd suspected it would.

The age group of owning a gun was getting younger. The youth were now banging from eleven. As far as I knew, things were going fine until this boy he had sold an assortment of weapons to got arrested. I remember him panicking and saying he thought the kid might grass him up. So we decided to try and get rid of it all. Of course, keeping a few of our favourites just in case someone decided to try and attack, we would be ready. It was like that in the hood. You never know when something is gonna kick off so you always have to live on standby.

Only if they knew. I smirked. The only thing that pissed me off is that my step-mum had to go through the whole search as well. She was still in bed when they came and ~~took~~ ten minutes to open her bedroom door to them. Even then they had to get a black female officer to talk her into letting her in. It's funny, because up to this day I think of what would have happened if they had knocked the door off when my dad was still there. I knew if they tried to rough up my dad it would have really got nasty. I would die for my dad, plain and simple, so thank God he left before they came.

Two hours later, still hand-cuffed besides my brother, the police ended their search and had words with my step-mum. They told her to kick us out, convincing her that letting us go would give us a sense of responsibility. In other words: You can't do anything for them now. Let them be responsible for their own lives. Abandon them. They left, taking a few knifes and baseball bats since they didn't get what they'd came for, an unknown quantity of fire arm.

That was stupid, I thought. *How you gonna tell my step-mother to kick me out when this was my release address?* If I couldn't stay here then I'd still be in prison serving out the remainder of my sentence. I was only back at my step-mother's place because it was the only way I could get parole. Plus, both the prison and probation system thought my parents would keep me out of trouble. In my opinion, placing me back in Hackney got me caught right back up in the mix. After the raid, me and Klinton agreed it was time to move out as the current circumstances had shook my step-mother up something bad.

CHAPTER: NINETEEN |

Monday morning two days after the raid, both me and Klinton went down to the housing department, filled out the forms and waited our turn to be interviewed to see if we met Hackney's requirements to be re-housed. It must have been Klinton's lucky day because he was offered a hostel in Dalston Market. It was filled with crack heads and drunk people, but they had a room and Klint was just glad to move out of his mum's house. Plus, being that he was twenty-five, he met the criteria and was given the keys. For me, it wasn't going to be so easy.

"Because you have been released to your parent's house you could be sent back to prison if you breach those conditions," I was told by the lady who interviewed me.

"Look, what have I got to do? Because right about now I need to get out of where I'm at now," I began to explain.

"You need to speak with your probation officer or if you change your address without them knowing ..." I got it, I could be sent back to prison. It seemed like every option I chose led to prison, but luck was on my side. When it came to my relationship with my probation officer, we had already known each other before

I went to prison. She was from the Ends and at the time was seeing an old friend of mine.

"I understand your concerns and I have no obligations toward you having a change of address. As long as you make it your priority to contact me regarding your housing status and at no time must you make yourself unavailable." I was pleased that my probation officer agreed that moving out of my step-mum's house and out of the estate could give me the opportunity I needed to take heed of the options presented to me. She assured me that if I found somewhere she would do everything possible to help me resettle. So sure enough, I returned to Hackney council day after day. For two whole weeks I sat in the baitest place in Hackney seeing people I knew, girls from back in the day. I said to myself, *if by the following Friday I don't get somewhere I'm going to rob any and everyone and rent privately.*

It was like my ritual sitting in the housing, calling the same numbers on the same sheet of paper I was given the day before. By Wednesday I must have been wearing my *"Don't fuck with me hat"* because as I walked through the doors, I was assisted by the manager, who informed me that she would be assessing my application.

Quite perky and bubbly, Loraine and I got on just fine. I kept it real with her.

"Look, Gwenton, I ain't gonna lie. I can't help you today, but come back on Friday and I'll have something for you then." I was elated. Now, finally I could return home to tell my dad and step-mum that come Friday I'd be ghost. They just didn't understand why it was taking me so long to be housed when it had taken Klinton only a day. I tried to keep out of their way, mainly sticking to my room when I was home. It felt like the day I moved out all over again. I wasn't wanted there.

Looking half-asleep and half decent as to be preserved as sleeping rough, first thing Friday morning I made my way to the housing and waited for Loraine. She turned up after an hour and immediately took photocopies of all my documents then returned for a bit of chat. I gathered she was trying to get to know me before she told me the good news. So I smiled and went along with her until she told me what I wanted to hear.

"Right. Where were we? Sorry, Gwenton, but we can't help you." My heart sank the moment the words rolled off her tongue. I could have died on the spot and she could see it on my face.

"Wait, I'm not finished. I can't promise you anything, but I know someone that may be able to." I listened as she went on to explain about an anti-gangs project called Makeda Weaver.

"His name is Alton Bell, and he's currently the manager of a new project that works alongside the housing association, Shian. Take this." She handed me a business card. "Alton Bell is a really down to earth person. Call him, Gwenton," she stressed before being called away.

I called Alton as soon as I left the housing office and he sounded as cool as Loraine said. Alton said he would help me get a flat. I could tell by his voice that he was an older Black man. I placed him in the same age group as my dad. He gave me the address to the Shian housing association and the directions to his office inside the building.

"Can you meet me on Monday, Gwenton? Is that good for you? Say 11 A.M.?" Alton asked.

I was filled with excitement when I got off the phone. The Makeda Weaver project sounded interesting and Alton had given me hope. I was feeling positive until I remembered that I would have to go home and relay the news of me not being able to move until Monday. Sometimes I wondered, *why couldn't I have a loving family who'd miss me when I was gone? A mother who wanted her son near and a father who put his child before his woman?*

I met Alton the following Monday and introduced myself as Que. Alton got straight down to business explaining what the Makeda Weaver project was all about and how it could be beneficial for a person like me.

145

"Here, Que." Alton said, and handed me a booklet. "Read this. It's about the project and what services we provide the community."

"The Makeda Weaver project offers young men the opportunity and support to change their life. If they are involved with gangs, guns, and violence we will redirect their life path. With nearly twenty years experience of working with ex-offenders and those at risk of offending, in our team we are well-placed to make a difference. Our team has backgrounds from probation and youth justice, youth work and sports. Our ethos is to mentor support to ex-offenders with the safety of the community. We are still very much in touch with the streets and believe this to be important in the way we work to improve conditions for BME communities. We offer cognitive lifestyle group work programmes addressing: offering victim empathy and social skills tools; solution focused one-to-one sessions; one-to-one mentoring sessions; life skills; budgeting and housing support; housing and relocation options; training; work experience and employment opportunities." For the first time in a long while I was interested in something other than the gang life.

It was still bright and early in the morning but I listened intensely as Alton explained what Makeda Weaver was and how the project worked.

"We are not just about providing young gentlemen like yourself properties, you will be required to participate in the project, produce a CV, and be active in looking for work." I was all for the change. After all, I was already enrolled in college for the following year. Within a week of our meeting, Alton called me with an offer of a flat in Highgate.

It's out of the ends, perfect! I couldn't thank Alton enough and I accepted the offer. He promised, he, along with the rest of the Makeda Weaver team would support me with relocating. Alton would call me and do home visits to make sure I was coping okay. I respected him as he would try to look out for me, but after a few months I could tell there was something going on. He would hardly call or come around. One day Alton called me with some bad news. He told me that he was leaving the Makeda Weaver project and that a new manager would be moving in to take his place.

The project inspired me and I tried to set up my own project called "Crying Sons." It was a cause for mothers of the victims who died through gun crime. There was already a project called Mothers against Guns, so I set up my project to sell DVDs with tributes and stories from all parts of the borough, but I should have known it wouldn't work. It proved virtually impossible to record all the areas of Hackney on my DVD. Some people were still holding bad feelings towards me for things I had done or over killings that took place when I was in prison. In the hood when someone gets killed from the other side, people always labelled everyone the murderer. We all knew the rules though and we lived dealing with the consequences of the actions of others. I knew that both parties were entitled to protect their set, so I had to fall back on my plans to protect myself, from the enemy and from breaching the terms of my parole.

Trying to go legitimate, I saw ninety percent of my old friends get killed or return to prison. It was hard going from a once most envied person in the hood because you were paid, to not being able to buy a pair of trainers, falling behind on the water bill, and falling into debt. The streets were always watching you and people love to talk. Three years ago I was driving a Golf GTI fresh out the show-room and a couple of months ago I was seen walking to the job centre. These were hard times for me. I was tempted to go back to my old ways needing to make some quick cash. It was around then that I formed a relationship with Leanne.

***

Before I was kicked out of Aylesbury HMP prison I became friends with a guy named Camron. We met ironically because we were located to the same wing, that and we both shared a common interest in rap music. Travelling around the county from prison to prison I had two note books full of rhymes before I was transferred to Aylesbury but when me and Cam, went at it together we were a good team. Cam was like a brother to me during the time we'd spent banged up. He was released from jail four months before me, we'd swapped numbers and promised to keep in touch, which we did.

Detaching myself from my usual crowd seemed harder than I'd anticipated at first. Kat called me occasionally and so did Klinton when he had a move that he knew I couldn't afford to turn down. I was sill unemployed and struggling financially. But like I'd agreed I called Camron who now lived in Walthamstow and soon found something positive to avert my attention to.

"Yo. I wondered when I was gonna be hearing from you!" Camron said when I called him, months after I'd been released.

"Don't watch nothing Fam. I been out for a hot minute but you know how it goes I had to find my way."

"Yeah I hear dat." Cam chuckled. He knew exactly what I meant. We caught up on the phone and he explained that he'd face much of what I was going through since his release four month before mine. He'd been homeless and faced situations where he could have easily ended up re-offending had it not been for his passion for music.

"Look, you should come down to Stow (Walthamstow) and see the studio I built in my yard (house). Lay down a few tracks. Even make an album." Walthamstow is a twenty minute drive from Hackney, a small distance to travel to see and old friend. But I was on a driving ban and refused to take public transport into another area let alone my own. I'd just have to wait until I had enough money to buy a bike.

The thought of standing in the booth and tearing up the mic had me hyped and put me back in my graphing zone. There were always ways on the block to make a quick couple of grand. If you needed any more than that you had to go out of town. I held off on visiting Carmon for a few weeks and focused on making money to obtain a bike which I desperately needed to get me around town safely. I was serious about my Makeda Weaver project and word on the streets was I had sort housing and refuge from a government organisation that worked closely with the police. I no longer had that brotherly connection with the Holly Street boys or LOM; instead I rolled with a selective few. Those who'd kept it real with me from day dot, this was because of fear people smiled nervously in my face and showed me fake love while behind my back they were unloyal. I was learning how to read people. Being vulnerable as a child, I found ways to see the inner person rather than the exterior they wore. It was sad. I was now looking at the faces of some of my closest friends and saw they were scared. Scared and ashamed to be. It's a difficult time when someone from the streets decides he wants out of the life. The people around him think only about themselves. *We've done so much dirt together, what if he rats me out? If I get hit will he be down? Will he sell me out for a better life? How am I gonna make money without him?*

It couldn't have taken me more than three weeks before I was able to purchase a motor bike. I paid £2500 for a R6 Yamaha and linked up with Trav that very day to see Camron and his studio.

"Come ere fam!" Camron embraced me when I made it to his house late that afternoon.

"It's good to see you brouv." He said looking over my shoulder at Trav.

"Cam. This is Trav, my boy. He's cool." I reassured him.

Camron respected my word and pounded Trav before we entered his home. It was a good feeling to be free with someone who was incarcerated with you.

"I know you wanna see the studio right?" Cam clapped his hands excitedly.

"Well I didn't come to watch TV." I joked with him.

"Hear you. It's down here," leading us down stairs Camron and I talked about how we used to write rhymes in prison and how he said when he got released he was going to build a studio in the

149

first place he got and work of a joint that would get his name out there. I wasn't surprised that months later here we were.

"Come in, come in." Camron brought us into a large back room with like he'd said he'd converted into a studio. It was pretty impressive with all the technicals, amps and speakers. Cam came to life in this room; it was obvious that this was his forte. But I can't even lie I was feeling myself too. I couldn't wait to get in the booth and lay down something fresh. Trav took a seat between two girls that were already in the studio, messing about on the mic and talking loud.

"Gimme dat get out of there!" Camron played with the lightest of the girls, snatching a mic out of her hands and playfully chucking her out the booth.

"My boy Que's gonna show us what he's got. Do your thing Que." He said holding the door to the booth open for me to step inside.

"Go Que. whoop, whoop." The cute girls hyped me up. Being in the studio made the whole dream feel like it was real. I took my jacket off and hung it over the end of a chair before I entered the booth.

"Gimme a beat den." I held my hands up and shouted although I couldn't yet be heard until the mic was on.

"Wait superstar, lemme just fix up all this stuff these damn girls been playing with." Cam said switching on switches and fiddling with tabs.

"You ready?"

"Yeah, drop it." I said confident. I looked through the glass and saw I had Trav and Cam's two female friend's attention.

> *Done stood amongst these four cornered walls with bars,*
> *These times my boys on road driving nice cars,*
> *Drinking tequila shots in bars,*
> *But I don't mind, when I land it's my time,*
> *Can't come back to prison for guns, drugs or a knife,*
> *Or cos a guy on road is sexing my wife*

I need a nice house,
A nice car,
A nice bike,
A nice chrome glock, to protect my life
In case of if my best friend wants to take my life,
The thought of that brings tears to my eyes,
Done live the hard life, the prison short days and long nights,
Done seen the wing fights now back on the road where the guns
light,
I've given enemies a second chance of life,
Cause I'm at work doing a nine to five.

I went in hard with the hook.

Street life ain't a joke; you can die as a beginner
Want to be a bad-man
Super-man killer
The youth got that hollow tip shank or bullet that will kill ya

I smiled when I saw the one of the girls get up swaying her hips feeling my bars. I continued.

I don't care like Blair the Prime-Minster,
I make your mum say halleluiah,
As I'm putting holes in yah
Because I'm badder than most
Don't brag I don't boast
Burn up your face like toast
Disappear like Casper the friendly ghost

Street life ain't a joke; you can die as a beginner
Want to be a bad-man
Super-man killer
The youth got that hollow tip shank or bullet that will kill ya

This time when I spat the hook I had back-up; the girl feeling my

151

bars was spitting it with me.

I stepped out the booth feeling like a star was born.

"Fuck me, Que! That was some good shit you laid down in there. I'm feeling that shit." Camron jumped from his chair excitedly and put his arm around my shoulder. It felt good to get all that off my chest and have people acknowledge that my rhymes were good. But deep down I knew I could never own this dream it would be impossible for me to make it big. I had done too much dirt to let the hole world know my whereabouts, there would be a fare chance I'd be killed at a show if one of my pass enemies or victims saw my name on a flyer.

"Yeah man you gotta let me record that." I said pulling him to the side. The cute girl that had been singing along with my hook was sweating me hard. I could tell. She was doing that whole eye contact thing girls did when they wanted you to come over and ask them their name.

"Cam, who's that's girl" I asked nodding my head discreetly in her direction.

"Fam. that's my cousin." Cam told me. Immediately I took her out of my mind I didn't want to disrespect Camron. Her friend was just as nice as, dark-skinned with big a bright eye that called you.

Trav and I spent the rest of the day chilling at Camron's house with his cousin and her friend who had told me her name was Leanne. She was cool, so when we left and Camron walked me and Trav to the door I asked him to hook us up and he said it was done. I never knew what Cam said to Leanne but I was glad she called me later that night.

CHAPTER: TWENTY |

In all honesty I wasn't looking for a relationship. I was looking for a companion, a female I could spend time with when I wasn't on the roads or chilling with my boys. I hadn't smelt the scent of a woman or even been sexually close to a female for 3 years. Worst than that I was lonely; I'd had plenty of time to be solo in jail and decided I'd take my chances with Leanne when she called.

"Hey Que. I hope you remember me." Leanne said when I answered her call, letting it ring over three times. I had just ridden back from Trav's place and put my key in the lock when Leanne called.

"Who's this?" I said not recognising her number.

"It's Leanne. We met at Cam's house; he gave me your number and told me that you wanted to talk to me."

"Oh yeah, he did?" I toyed with her.

"Yeah he did."

"Well he was right. I do wanna chat to you, I kinda thought we was feeling each other today and I thought that if you weren't up to anything later we could go raving have a drink. Nothing sexual doh" she laughed, as did I.

"Yeah, that's cool. I ain't got any plans, what you wanna do?"

"Well..." I told her "I was thinking about passing through some rave in Kings Cross, you can follow me if you want."

"Ok, what time you leaving?" she asked. We made plans for her to meet me at my place at eleven, and we would call a cab to take us to the rave where I told her we was only passing through so we'd stay there two hours max.

I gave Leanne my address before we said good bye and quickly made a start of cleaning the mess out of my room. I'd always been domesticated but I hand a knack of tardiness. I grabbed a handful of unfolded clothes and stuffed them in my wardrobe. I now had the task of washing the small amount of dishes in the sink and making my bed, all before I had a shower and got dressed before Leanne arrived.

Brrrrrrr

The buzzer to my door rang out just as I buttoned the last button on my shirt. I grabbed the D&G aftershave off my dresser and sprayed my upper body then checked myself in the mirror before I went to get the door.

"Hi Que," Leanne fluttered her eyes at me when I opened the door. She looked so cute standing in the door way in a tight black jeans and silver stilettos, the opened toe kind. Leanne was great company, we hit it off the moment I invited her inside. She was a few years younger than me and had no knowledge of my reputation which would work out great between us because I wouldn't have to watch my back in her company. Before we knew it, it was quarter to one and we'd long forgotten we were going out. We could have still made the club but the reality was that I don't think we would have ever left my flat that evening. I would have been kidding myself if I thought I could roll up in a rave with a female and no army.

"You sure you don't mind not going to the rave?" I asked Leanne as we sat comfortably on my sofa. She had taken off her shoes and wore a pair of my socks to keep her feet warm. We just chilled like that for ages, talking about our families, upbringing and what we wanted to be doing in the future. Neither of us were tired,

154

I guess we were enjoying each other's company alike and could have continued that way for hours.

"Nah, I don't mind. It's nice hanging out with you. I'm enjoying myself." Leanne answered.

"Yeah, me too." I softly whispered as I leaned towards her and kissed her neck. Leanne didn't reject my attachment instead her gentle breathing let me know that it was ok for me to finish what I was about to start. I moved up closed to her Kissing my way to her lips. Kissing and touching she laid on her back while I lay on top of her wondering if she could feel my hard dick resting on a soft spot between her legs. Leanne didn't stop me she didn't seem like the type of girl that would let a man get his without getting hers first. She fumbled with my jeans button's and when she was finally able to undo each one she dove in a released what I had been trying to maintain from the moment she walked through the door.

"Yeahh. Ummm. Yeah." I moaned as Leanne began to genitally stroke my manhood to steel. I tilted her head to the side and began leaving passion marks on her neck leading down to her breasts. Leanne shrieked in pleasure, the back of her legs was pushed up against the end of the couch. She knew all she had to do was throw herself back and I'd fall on top of her but she wanted something more that the average love making. She wanted to fuck, I read her mind. And swiftly turned her around positioning her on her knees at the foot of the couch.

"Ah shit." she yelled as I entered her from behind, I wrapped a handful of her long bouncing curls in my fist and gripped it tight while I worked myself in and out of her love tunnel releasing inside of her years of sexual tension.

"You wanna stay?" I asked her as we lay entwined, both trying to catch our breath.

"I can't, I gotta go home." she said. Then I remembered she was younger than me and lived at home with her parents.
Leanne caught a cab home in the early hours of the morning. She did something to me. And after that night we spent many together.

***

"Que, glups lib bled, his blon," Klinton said.

"Whoa?" I mumbled, trying to make out what Klinton was trying to tell me. Me and Leanne had been watching DVDs in bed the night before and crashed when I heard my phone vibrating under my pillow. I looked on the screen with my eyes half opened as the light from the phone blinded me. It was 9 minutes to six.

"Poops is blon," Klinton said.

"What?" I asked. I didn't understand.

"He's gone. Poops is gone!" he repeated.

"Well, that's the way it goes, init?" I replied, thinking Poops had been arrested by the police.

"No, Que, he's gone. He got licked down last night and Green Eyes got hit, too." I turned over in the bed facing the ceiling. My first thought was revenge. Poops was an old and very dear friend to me. We'd been tight since primary school. Green Eyes was Poop's step brother so I had heart for both of them.

I'd been woken out my sleep and couldn't remain still. I remember going into the bathroom and sitting on the toilet seat as Klinton filled me in on how it went down. Straight away, I began to think of suspect's to seek revenge on and couldn't sit down any longer. I found anger brewing in me from within that place I'd tried so hard to keep contained.

"Klinton let me call you back. I'll call you later." I ended the call like that. *How many people am I gonna have snatched away from me?* I already had a few suspects in my head and I was ready to do what I thought was expected of me, being a loyal friend. Unable to rest, I stayed up until 10 A.M. watching TV until I couldn't take it anymore.

"Where you going?" Leanne rolled over in the bed and rubbed her eyes. I'd tried my best not to wake her, but turning the bedroom light on had cause her to stir. Now she was fully awake, looking at me strangely as I stood fully dressed about to make an exit.

"I need to use the phone." I said, shutting the front door

behind me. I had a mobile, which I'd recently topped up, but I didn't want to call anyone off my personal number. It was just how it was. When someone got killed, police tapped people's phones all the time. I looked both ways down the road, flipped on my hood, and stepped in the phone box.

"Is it true?" I needed to hear it from someone else to make sense of what I had been told, so I called Temper, another old school friend who we'd grown up with.

"Yeah," he said after an awkward silence. I could have fainted there in the phone box. I felt lost, but knew someone had to pay. Suddenly, I felt the murderous feeling come over me. It's when your emotions take over your normal way of thinking and makes you want to hurt or kill people. It takes years of losing close friends to learn to control this feeling. The next day I went to meet his stepbrother, Green Eyes, who accused me of having beef with Poops, but I didn't take it as a diss. I had a large amount of respect for him and I knew losing a brother had affected him emotionally. His mind was clouded, but I still had to ask.

"What's the deal? Who you think did it?"

"I don't even wanna think about it right now. This is some real madness, Que, but I know without a doubt it was dem Lordship fuckers and ..."

"And what?" I'd started to get hyped because Green Eyes had confirmed those who I felt would be responsible. Someone had to pay for Poops' death and if Green Eyes knew the culprit, I wanted to know.

"Shit's all fucked up right now." I watched as Green Eyes words came out his mouth, inhaling deeply before he spoke.

"We got fam' in Lordship, brouv, so if we going to war we gotta be ready to face some complications, plus ..."

"Plus what?" I was beginning to grow impatient. I wanted to deal with Poops' killer *now*!

"My baby mum's fucking one of dem, init? What's his name? LS. Dat boy dat people are claiming I shanked up." I couldn't believe what I was hearing. People had no loyalty, I shook my head.

"What happened?" I took a seat on the stairs and asked Green Eyes.

"Well, I can't be too sure, but people been saying that them youths was trying to hit me after what went down between me and him when I caught my baby's mother and him fucking." *I could kill that bitch*, I thought, but then I'd be caught in a catch twenty-two. I couldn't hurt Green Eye's baby mother. She was the mother of his son, but on the other hand, someone had to pay. She was a traitor; she'd sold out her baby's father for a few nights of passion, which resulted in the murder of one of my best friends.

"Let me move to her, brouv." I stood to my feet.

"Fam', sit down. You mad. You can't move to her, dats my baby's mother." I sat back down. I believed in the "everyone gets hurt rule" be it mother, brother, sister or friend. I wasn't happy with Green Eye's wishes, but I respected them.

A swarm of people turned up to give their condolences and pay respect to Poops and his family. It was weird because every once in a while I'd spot someone in the crowd who I knew rep the other set. Or worse, was down with the Lordship boys. I just couldn't understand it and it made me feel uncomfortable. I was still on parole and felt like I was going to end up getting a life sentence if I stuck around. So I made a quiet exit and took a back seat. I wanted to see if anyone else would set the pace then I would do my thing.

Sugar, Poops' older brother, was the only person that put work in. Everyone else just pretended they were down for Poops and many of those people still pretend today. I mean, don't get me wrong, Hackney is a small place and at times it can seem as if everyone is linked in some way through family, friends, or money and drugs.

Still, I couldn't believe Poops was gone. During the past six months he and I had grown close, so close that I'd given him my R6 motor bike. He said he didn't feel it was wise or safe for him to walk around the area on foot. There were rumours going around the borough that there was a hit out on him over the murder of a Turkish boy, who's body was thrown in the canal. Poops had been trailed for the incident and had been recently released. When we became tight, growing up he was one of the youngest boys allowed to hang around with us. He didn't need to fight to prove himself because his older brother was well known and respected in the area. They were also related to the Brissett family, who were well known for making money. Poop was welcomed into our clique with open arms and he fit in just right. He sported a long scar across his head that looked like the result of a serious operation as a kid. So, we all thought if he was hit on the head there was a possibility he would die. It was a complete shock for me when I was released from jail and heard stories about Poops stabbing people in the streets.

Poops was my boy to the end. We did a lot of dirt together, and had beef with the same people, the L.O.R.D boys who resided in the Lordship Estate. We dealt with death threats daily. They were still pissed about the killing of their Turkish friend, and since Poops went to prison for his murder they thought it was only right he should pay. A life for a life is how it was on the roads. I was cool with one of the Olders from Lordship, a guy called Smithy. He always had my back, but I had to put our friendship on hold. His boys had stabbed Klinton during our feud and being friends with the enemy could cost you your life.

With no disregard for the family of his victim, Poops set out to attack the L.O.R.D Boys any chance he got. Yeah, I was still on parole, but I got down with him because I wanted to see if he was as real as I'd heard he was. And sure enough he was realer than most of the people I'd ever done dirt with. Never scared to get his hands dirty on his own, I saw Poops cut open a man's stomach on the streets, causing his insides to bulge through the gash in his flesh.

I remember the last time I saw Poops, about five of us went on a bike ride through Essex where Kat lived. Naturally, we were all excited. Neither of us knew what the inside of Kat's house was gonna look like. We knew that with the type of money he was robbing off people he could have owned a mansion, but he didn't. Instead, he owned a large white house with a single garage painted white inside and out. It suited him and he knew it.

Poops, Kat and the boys I rolled with played computer games on Play Station 3 for hours, but not me; I was never into computer games. So, soon I got bored and started complaining. It was an hour ride back to East London so after a while we left. All five of us were racing our bikes on the motor-way. It was fun, but that was when I decided it was the end of my riding days. I loved bikes, but some of the stunts we were pulling had me shook. I could see that either I'd end up causing a serious accident in traffic or die in a crash. The adrenaline rush I got when I revved the engine was now replaced with fear. All I saw now were the dangers.

Finally, after a considerable amount of months without any contact from Makeda Weaver, I got a phone call from a member of staff informing me that I had a new housing officer. He wanted us to meet up and touch base to see if there was anything they could help with. After five and a half months with not even so much as a newsletter, I was reluctant to pay any mind to Makeda Weaver's concerns. But then I remembered Alton and what he had told me about the project and then I thought about Poops. I said to myself, *I'll go to the meeting and see what this new guy's saying, but if I ain't feeling him I'm gone and they ain't seeing me again.*

I turned up at the meeting fifteen minutes early and was acquainted with Leon and Richard, two guys dressed in suits who sat in the meeting room. Neither of them looking much older than me. I could tell they were both nervous when I walked in and took my seat around the table. Dressed in my usual attire, black jacket and dark blue jeans I had both hands deep in my pockets and held an expression on my face that read, "Get to the point or I'm out."

"Hi, I'm Richard." The first man held out his hand and shook mine firmly. He was a stocky kind of guy, bald headed but very confident. Richard had dark brown skin, much darker than mine and smiled every time he spoke.

"Gwenton, right?" He let go my hand and introduced his partner, Leon, who sat relaxed in his chair.

"Yeah." I shifted in my seat as Richard tried to break the ice. He was trying to act cool, but I wasn't buying it. *Right in ten minute's I'm kicking.* I looked at the clock on the wall in front of me and was sure that Richard and Leon were pretty decent guys, but I had other things on my mind.

After 4 four months of dating Leanne had announced she was pregnant, I was about to stand and make up some excuse for my departure when another short, dark-skinned trendy looking black guy walked into the meeting room catching my attention. He had long six-inch black hair that he'd twisted at the end like he was trying to grow dread locks.

I liked this dude. I smiled as I listened to Steven Joseph tell me his life story. He'd grown up in Stratford and knew quite a few people that I knew from the ends. If anything, he knew more. He'd been acquainted with some of the hardest men I'd heard of and was friends with some real gangsters. *If he knows them and they respected him then he must be cool,* I said to myself, admiring him as he spoke.

From then on Steve and I formed a friendship.

I had a baby on the way, it was so unreal. As Leanne's stomach started to stretch I got more and more excited to meet my child. I didn't just want to be the man who helped produce him; I wanted to be the man to provide for him, physically and emotionally. I wanted to give him everything my parents failed to give me, security, love, support, affection and most of all a dad to be proud of. Adamant that I wasn't going to let my child down, I was still desperately trying to fall back on my feet. With no job, no qualifications, and no real source of income coming in, I was tempted to hit the roads and continue the reputation I'd earned years ago.

The saying "Great minds think alike" couldn't have been

more than true. No sooner than I'd hit the streets, I got a phone call from Kat saying he had a big move and he wanted to put me on.

It was late the following evening when I drove to Newington Green to meet Kat. We sat outside parked in our cars, him driving a blue BMW convertible and me sporting a black BMW compact I'd bought with the money I'd acquired from small robberies. We spaced our cars apart, giving us driving space in case we had to make a quick getaway. We didn't speak in our cars. Instead, I followed Kat up the road where he laid out the instruction to the move.

Kat rubbed his hands together. "This ain't a robbery. It's something different," he explained. "I know some business man from the city. He used to buy crack off me back in the day and a couple of week's back he touched base with me about something he wanted handled."

"How much is he paying?" I asked, thinking only of what I was going to make off this move. It wasn't out of the ordinary for Kat to ring me up and try and get me on a movement with him, but most of the time I'd decline. For one, I was on parole and two, which should have been number one; I didn't trust anyone when it came to committing an offence. I was a one man show. I wasn't going to snitch on myself.

"Listen, Que." Kat stopped walking and turned to face me. He was serious. "My guy is a joint partner of a big city firm and he wants his partner off the planet so he ain't got to go through the trouble of buying him out. You know these city guys are crazy." He laughed. "Anyhow, he's gonna drop fifteen g's on it. He offered the job to me, but I just had to holler at you 'cause I know you been hurt for a little while and I wanted to help you out, you know, get you back on your feet." I appreciated the love Kat was showing me, but at the same time I wondered why Kat didn't just do the hit himself. *Why would he turn down the opportunity to earn fifteen grand?*

"This how it's gonna go down." He got hyped. "You gone have to meet up with this white business man next week, so make sure you dress smart. They gonna show you the location and the target, but in all, he just wants to meet up with you to see if you're up to it. I know you gonna be cool, but this ain't nothing like we done before." Kat was right; we'd done a lot of dirt before but never committed murder. At a time like this I wished I had that feeling that made me want to take a life, but I was soon to find out that what I wanted to kill for would be the same thing I wanted to live for.

"I'm gonna give you half the money next week up front and the rest you get when the job's done," Kat said before he put his car in drive and sped off. Now, I wasn't worried about killing this random person. The thought of the money just filled me with excitement. My hands began to sweat and I thought about calling Kat back and asking him if we could just deal with this man tonight so I could get paid, but I didn't. I held my tongue; I knew it would seem unprofessional. I always tried to play the calm and smart guy so people took me seriously, and it worked, but I wasn't no fool., I'd been shitted on by Dark Man, snitched on by Orbery, and robbed by Super being that my gut told me to be weary. I contacted Riggs, right hand man to the most feared and talked about Rasta man in London.

"Riggs, what's good?"

"Ah 'ho dis?" Riggs must have looked at the caller I.D and not recognized the number.

"It's Que. Riggs, what's good?"

"Nuttin' cuz, wha' blow? Everything is everything. What can I do for you?"

"I need your advice on something."

"Shoot."

"How much does it cost to do a hit?"

Riggs went silent for a second. Honestly, so did I. People did hits everyday and I know my question didn't come as a surprise. But I think he was surprised that the question came from me. I'd known Riggs from the time I came to England and he'd never known me to be a killer.

"It's fifteen gib for someone you know and a twenty-five for someone you don't." *Twenty-five gib*, I thought to myself. I couldn't believe Kat was trying to rob me of ten grand. I was so deep in thought that I didn't hear Riggs still talking on the other end of the phone.

"How you ain't come check me since you land, road? You good doh, yeah?" he continued, changing the subject and not questioning me about my reasons for asking for such information.

I hung up the phone feeling like a mug. I thought about confronting Kat, but I thought, you know what? Kat's always been dodgy (sneaky). Let him have that because he's not having any of my fifteen grand.

CHAPTER: TWENTY-ONE |

Kat called me the Sunday before the Wednesday I was to meet up with these unknown businessmen. He told me that once I was shown the location and target I would be given half of my payment up-front. Once I'd taken it, there was no turning back.

"What you expect to be shown who the target is and then decide that you don't wanna do the hit. Nah, it ain't that. Once you take that money it's a done deal 'cause whether you kill dude or not, he's gotta go. And if shit goes wrong, we looking suspect."

"I hear you," I said, understanding where he was coming from. I knew that these guys we were working for could easily put fifteen grand on my head if I didn't go through with the hit and they felt uncomfortable about me knowing their initial plan.

"So what, you gonna drop your man a nice change for setting you straight?" Kat then had the nerve to ask.

"How much?" I asked him in a calm manner, trying to contain my digression.

"Come on, man, just a nice change. I'm dead too. You know how it is out here." I imagined him smiling on the other end of the phone seeing as he had already robbed me for ten grand. *Don't be greedy, Que,* I told myself calculating my loss. Ten grand would be enough to get me back on my feet. I wasn't worried about my present financial situation, but that of the future. I could barely provide for myself when times got hard and now I had Leanne and our unborn child to think of.

"Look, I'm gonna front you five grand," I said, knowing that that was as fair as it could get.

"Que, five grand! You're killing me. Seven -fif."

"Seven-fif, brouv. You're milking it. I got a baby on the way," I stressed, hoping he would just take the bait and let it be.

"Alright cool five grand." Again, I sensed him smiling. He'd made a quick fifteen grand at my expense and though I was angry and unable to understand his reasons behind crossing me, I anticipated getting paid and was excited to be back in the game.

Two nights before the hit, I came home and sat on the edge of the bed going over the events that would take place in the days ahead. *Was I making the right move?* With just one month before my child was born, and just ninety one pounds a fortnight as income from the job centre, I became more compelled by the thought of landing back on my feet. I watched Leanne as she waddled in, all podgy and swollen in her night shirt and embraced me when she got close.

"Baby," I began as I proceeded to tell her my plans., I was sure that she would be satisfied with my efforts and proud that her man had come through, seeing as we were living in my one bedroom flat in High Gate in North London.

"Do you really need the money?" She fell from my grasp and looked me dead in the eye. "I thought we were nice for money. What if you get caught? You'll go back to jail and you'll never see this baby." She placed my hand on our moving child. I thought, *it's not like I could pull out now. I already had my half and I wasn't about to get killed for not carrying out the hit. People were relying on me to eat.*

"You do what you gotta do, Que, but if you're doing it 'cause you think we need this money, then we don't. So you don't have to put yourself at risk like that." I looked into Leanne's face and saw the sadness in her eyes. I knew that this woman, although not the first, had deep feelings for me. She was carrying my child and loving me all at the same time.

I couldn't convince Leanne that what I was doing was for the best because I was struggling to convince myself. I went to bed that night and dreamt of seeing myself killing a man dressed in a grey pinstriped business suite. I saw myself casually walk into his home and point a gun at his head. I watched his mother cry and heard her plea for his life, begging God to bring him back.

I awoke in a cold sweat and turned over to find Leanne in a deep sleep. She slept without a care in the world with her large stomach sticking out from under her night clothes. It hit me that I couldn't kill some random guy. I just couldn't put a price on a life. Sure, I tried to take out rival gang members, but that was war, either them or me. No amount of money could clear my conscience, but the pressure was on. I collected the seventy-five hundred pound advance and had even dipped into it a little, preparing for the arrival of my child that would be born any day soon.

The thought of my unborn child's life being taken away or harmed in any way as the consequence of my actions was the only thing strong enough to coax me into finding an alternative plan.

CHAPTER: TWENTY-TWO |

Everybody knew Mad Owen around Stokey; he was always on madness and held no regard for the law. Originally Klinton's friend, but quite acquainted with me, I knew his broke ass would jump at the opportunity to make a little change. In fact, Owen was the type of guy to kill a man just because his disregard for the law was that of his disregard for life. I remember when we were younger; he set fire to our front door as a joke nearly burning down our flat. The fire brigade had to be called to put out the blaze, and even then, seeing us being escorted onto the landing out of our smoke-filled landing gave him nothing but satisfaction.

I contemplated calling Owen. I knew he'd be on it, but putting him on would be taking a chance with his loyalty. He was unstable and incapable of following direct instructions.

"So, this is a sure thing, yeah?" Owen's eye lit up when we met up that afternoon in the flat's where I put him down on the hit. His five-feet-seven inch frame seemed to grow as he grew excited thinking about the seven and a half grand I'd offered him to do the job. I knew I was being just as cunning as Kat making money off my man, but I still needed my cut.

"Yeah, it's solid," I said, bringing him in. I now needed to inform Kat of the change of plans and I already knew he wouldn't be happy. Still, I said fuck it and called him when I left Owen just one day before the move.

I could tell by the change of the tone in Kat's voice that he was upset and maybe disappointed that I wasn't going to see the move out to the end. "I brought you on first 'cause I knew this was something you could handle. I could have got my links in west to deal with this, but I wanted to keep it in-house." He paused, probably smoking or wondering how my change in his plans would affect his cut.

"You know what? Don't watch that, Que. Just get your boy to call me and I'll make the connect. We got bigger things happening right now. If you think he's cool then I'm with it." Ending that call with Kat was like being able to retire, knowing I was coming out the game with my life if nothing more. I went home to Leanne feeling content our child would be born in less than two weeks and nothing was going to stop me from being there.

That night I went to sleep with my conscience clear. And as I slept, I wished Owen all the best as he prepared to take my place the following morning.

***

Like I said before, Owen found it almost imposable to follow direct instructions and thought it best that the hit was performed in a style to his liking.

Drunk and disorientated, Owen started his mission from the night before. As we slept comfortably in our beds, Owen was out creeping, stealing a number plate off a parked car to replace with the number plate on the car provided to him by Kat's connect, along with the tool he was to use to eliminate the target. *What a fool,* I thought the following day when I heard news that he'd been arrested that night having been caught driving around intoxicated in a car with a stolen number plate. The police had found him with a loaded fire arm in his possession. When he was pulled over he was said to have punched an officer in the face before trying to escape an already bad situation.

"That's bullshit!" Kat screamed at me when I told him what had happened to Owen. He was convinced that Owen had taken his cut and ditched.

"How can I believe your boy got arrested?" It took me about a week to convince Kat that Owen was being held in Brixton prison and that he would be spending four months there due to the circumstances of his arrest. As if that wasn't enough, I then had to vouch that Owen wouldn't grass up the people involved in organising the hit. Under normal circumstances I wouldn't put my mouth on anyone's loyalty, but I knew that I needed to tell Kat and his people what they wanted to hear. And if Owen did snitch then I'd just have to deal with the consequence when it happened.

Up to this day I never found out who the target was, nor did I care. Neither of us completed the job, Owen did his time silently and was home almost before his sentence had started. He'd spoken to no one about the hit, keeping my name out the mix when he was questioned by the police, allowing me to be present at my son's birth. I was glad that Owen was released and I felt guilty about his arrest.

My son was born a healthy seven pounds six ounces on January 29, 2007 and his birth was one of the biggest events in my life. When he was placed in my arms for the first time, I felt nothing but warmth. Taken back by how much he resembled me and mesmerised by his presence. His coo's melted my heart and for the first time ever, I loved. I loved him unconditionally, whole heartedly and knew that if there was ever a time, I would exchange my life for his. My only disappointment was that my mother would never get the chance to see her grandson. I felt that as her coffin was laid in the ground so was my ability to love. I gave thanks to be able to own that feeling again, but even more so for the feeling that stirred in me when I looked into my new born child's eyes.

Qwenton Sloley, just a few minutes old loved me back without question. I felt the connection the moment he was born. The new life I held in my hands depended on me. I didn't want him to grow up knowing I was on the roads robbing people. I'd been lying to myself, telling myself I was doing it for him, when in reality I was hooked on the excitement and the rush I got from the power I held over people. I was respected by both the people who claimed to love me and the people who hated me, too. Poops and Lamont's (Monty) death had proved that respect wasn't bullet proof, nor did it keep your enemies at bay. It wasn't going to be easy withdrawing myself from the crowd I worked so hard to become a part of, but Qwenton gave me motive to try. I grew up seeing my own father leave the house for work every morning. I watched his move from job to job trying to up his pay; things I thought were meaningless until Qwenton was born.

Yes, I still wanted respect. I wanted to be looked up to and admired. I thought about all the Younger's I welcomed into my world and all the Olders who'd welcomed me into theirs. I had a responsibility to others as well as my own. I swore on my knees in prison that I would come out and be good.

I was a parent now. I felt like I'd been welcomed into a secret world of joy and unexplainable love. Had my son not been born I would have without a doubt ended up back in prison, or would have considered taking the hit Kat had handed me. I would have still been running around the streets seeking revenge for my friends' deaths or for the wrongs people had done to me in the past. I had been given a second chance. Qwenton gave me a reason to live and achieve what people thought I couldn't.

It's who you are that matters. I smiled, holding my son thinking about my mother and her life here on earth. I understood that everybody's days were numbered and when we left, what is left of us is memories. Peoples thoughts, how they remembered us, and what we gave. I'd taken from my community what my family had taken from me, "Growth, progression, and hope."

CHAPTER: TWENTY-THREE |

After Qwenton was born, I found it difficult, but I buried some of my past and allowed my heart to warm towards the idea of being more acquainted with my mother's side of the family. At first it was overwhelming, quite a lot to take in, but I was happy that I had met them at last. Seeing them at my mother's funeral wasn't much of a meeting. Now I had a chance to introduce them to Qwenton.

I was the only missing member of my mum's family. They had all grown up together in Camden, which was strange, because when I started dealing drugs that was my location. Just five minutes away from where my Gran and all the other members of my family resided in Kentish Town.

Through recent visits I learnt that over the years Gran remarried to a man called, Mass Joe, who had children from his previous marriage with a woman who lived around the corner from them. They didn't have any children together so both their children grew up as one big family. It was then that I met my cousin, Kevin. He was from Mass Joe's side of the family, but was better known as the "Rude Boy" or the outcast.

Until a few years back, Kevin was as good as the boss of

Kentish Town. He was the man in their little village. He made a lot of money and liked nothing better than to show it off. It was through Kat that I learnt he had links with a lot of different white gangster families, who would give him anything he needed to make money or to protect himself.

Even though I knew I was connected to Kevin, I allowed Kat to involve me in a new plan that he was conjuring up. This time he told me he had a friend that could get me Kevin's number and once he did I should get close to him. Then we could rob him and if need be, kill him, but this all had to be done on the down low. Kevin had major links to the A Team in Islington, who were a vicious and relentless family.

Meeting Kevin for the first time I learnt very quickly that he was no longer the man that I was told he was. Like me, Kevin had had his time on the streets and he spoke with wisdom, teaching me how to take the first steps I needed to free myself from the streets.

"Cuz, listen. I wasn't supposed to say anything, but the reason I got in contact with you was because I was supposed to set you up to get robbed. Killed, if I had to," I admitted to him one afternoon while we hung out. I was spending a lot of time with Kevin though much of it was spent illegally. We bonded and I respected him. I could be sneaky to outsiders, but I wasn't about to stab my own family in the back.

Kevin laughed. "Que, you can forget all that Hackney crap. You're with your family now and as for you and this Kat I been hearing about, you need to drop him. I could make you rich!" he explained, not bothered by my confession. I felt it only right to adhere to Kevin's wishes and I soon dropped Kat. Our friendship turned sour, but truth be told, I made more money with Kevin in the six months I'd known him than I ever did in the years I'd known Kat. Kevin introduced me to other family members I had no idea I was related to Dennis'. They shared the same surname with my mother's family and were well known all over Hackney, Islington, and Camden. When I first came on the streets, they were the power force behind the Older London Fields Boys. Our Older

Holly Street Boys were scared of them. Kevin also told me Kat was using me, as his times on the roads were finished years ago. He was getting old and needed me to keep his name ringing in the streets.

Meeting my mother's family also acquainted me with Uncle Less, although really my cousin, I called him Uncle for respect as he was much older than me. Uncle Less was one of the most intelligent and loyal men I have ever met in my life and was well respected by businessmen all over London. He showed me how to conduct myself around rich powerful people. Some of the people I have come into contact with are beyond belief. It was like all my hard work had paid off. The hardest thing for me to deal with was the transition that Uncle Less took me through. He said, "Your street days are finished, Que 'cause I can only see you getting killed. You're a good yout. I'm gonna make you legal." Together we planned on owning a night club, but unfortunately, I didn't have the patience to complete all the paper work or attend the meetings. So eventually, I left him to it. He was upset with me for days, but I just wasn't used to that type of responsibility.

"To be a proper businessman you have to meet all the solicitors and partners and learn about the paper work and overheads at the same time." Uncle Less, like Kevin, didn't hold any feelings towards my decision to abort the night club business. Instead, he supported me with my unemployment by allowing me to help out in the club until something came my way. I worked there with him through the summer, keeping myself out of trouble and by winter I had received a phone call from Steven Joseph, the manager of Makeda Weaver.

"How have you been, Gwenton?" he asked me first off.

"I'm good," I explained, feeling good that this time I had something positive to relay back to the project. "I've been working with my family. It's nothing much, but I'm staying out of trouble and supporting my son, which is most important. Right!" I went on.

"Right, right. That's good to hear, Gwenton. I'm glad you

getting back on your feet. In fact, I called because I have a job vacancy come available and I wanted to know how you felt about me putting you forward for the job."

Hell yeah, I wanted to scream. Instead, I remained calm and listened as Steven filled me in about the position. "Now the post is initially for a mentor. It's thirty- six hours a week and pays above minimum wage."

"Sounds like just what you been waiting for to completely get you off the roads. You'll be getting paid good money, so you'll never need to extort or rob anyone again. If you decide to take this job I'll support you a hundred percent," Uncle Less told me when I asked for his opinion. I was elated that Steven had given me this chance. I couldn't believe I was going to be fully employed, working a nine to five dressed up in a shirt and shoes. It made me think the people at Makeda Weaver hadn't forgotten about me. They'd filled their end of the contract, now it was time for me to fill mine. What better way to do it than to mentor others just like me?

CHAPTER: TWENTY-FOUR |

In 2008, I worked alongside Steven on a lower end witness protection project put together by Southwark Council and a policeman from Scotland Yard. I was the first to work on the project and although Steven was my manager, he welcomed the added work and anticipated getting involved with the group getting his hands dirty here and there. I enjoyed Steven's company. He reminded me of all the nights we would work until 10 P.M. though most of the time I couldn't tell you where the time went. Steven and I would share stories of our own childhood and of the time we spent on the streets. Although he was ten years older than I, we had much to relate. I found out that he too had spent time in prison for armed robbery. We both at some point in our lives had been addicted to the calling of the streets. Both of us had been tempted by its treasures. Working alongside Steven allowed me to find a new rush, something the streets could never provide.

I remember the first client we had transferred over from Southwark. We housed him in Hackney the first day he was released from prison. The seventy pounds they'd given him he'd already spent on trainers. Still confused by the rules of incarceration, he was so filled with road rush that he must have forgotten that he needed money to eat. Like me, the streets were once his home and without his peers and supporters, he felt naked. I felt quite honoured when he called me bugging out one night after coming off a call. One of his boys alerted him that one of their team had been stabbed. That night I had to sleep on his floor just so he didn't return to South London to re-offend or worst get killed.

Joining the Project opened my eyes. I'd complained when my step-mother ordered take out for herself and Klinton and left me to provide for myself, but I was grateful I'd had the opportunity to learn certain skills. My client had no social skills and he was constantly relying on me. Things that I thought were easy like cooking and cleaning, even personal hygiene were things my client had to learn to be considered a stable member of the community.

"Que, I got this ready cooked Southern fried chicken and some easy cook rice. You still gonna show me how to cook this," he asked me during a home visit. I hadn't expected to be at his property after hours on this particular evening, but my work had now become my life. I truly believed that if I could give this man the support and attention I craved from others, he wouldn't re-offend. And most of all, he would have options, things I didn't know I had until it was almost too late.

"Yeah, that's a minor," I said, using the same street slang we'd grown up with. I noticed my clients respected me more when I was real with them. I never played the over educated mentor who frowned at their down falls. Instead, I made it a point to educate them on the struggles I faced in life, letting them know that they weren't alone and that there were people out there who cared.

"Okay, it says remove packaging and place in oven on baking tray for 45 minutes on gas mark 5."

"You know how to do that?"

"Yeah, course. Oven foods a minor." He raised his eye brows and we laughed. I was glad my client was beginning to follow instructions without assistance. Those were vital skills an individual needed to survive. We put the chicken in the oven and I showed him how to wash the rice using the cold tap water. I showed him how to use his hand to wash off the starch and gave him direct instructions to put it on a low fire. Nothing could go wrong, or so I thought.

My client was quite capable and I didn't want him to feel as if I was shadowing him all the time. So I retreated to the sitting room, leaving him alone to finish the rice and pre- heat the chicken in the oven.

It had been a long day for me. I'd been up since 7 A.M. on my feet all day and I had come to see him straight from work. It was now something to 8 P.M. I was tired, but trying to fight the sleep. I could hear this voice through my sleep saying, "You know what I fancy? Egg fried rice. I'm gonna dry this rice first, yeah."

"Wah," I mumbled before being fully awakened by the beeping sound of the microwave. I turned around to see him trying to put the pot into the microwave, but the handle couldn't fit.

"Stop! Are you mad?" I leaped off the sofa and grabbed the pot. "You are trying to kill us? You could have caused a fire." Without thinking I shouted at him like I was scorning a child.

"I was trying to dry the rice." He struggled at the time, not understanding what it was that he was doing wrong. I looked in the pot and couldn't help but laugh. He had cracked two eggs in the pot of half cooked rice and though it looked a hot mess, he was pleased with his achievement until I explained where he had gone wrong.

We laughed about that incident for hours and when I told Steven the next day we laughed for the whole week. I also had to teach him how to build up his confidence and to complete his self-risk assessment. Knowing what areas not to go when moving around in Hackney because of gang affiliation was a must. The borough was thriving with gangs and gang members, some not very far from his home.

"Sometimes I feel like I would have been better off staying in Southwark because at least I knew the gangs I was living with," my client expressed to me on one of his down days. "I guess the only good thing about being relocated is that I ain't got to constantly watch my back or walk with a knife for my own protection." To hear that felt good. I had managed his risk for the time he was with us, and at the same time was building a good relationship with the inspector from Scotland Yard in charge of overseeing the project.

For the first time I had the privilege of being trusted with confidential information about clients the project catered to. I learnt how to keep information to myself. I was now working on a level I'd never been on before. Being a part of the Makeda Weaver project and working alongside Scotland Yard made me feel like I was a part of the CIA, I got a lot of hassle from my old gang members whose lives were still on the streets. Mainly because I was now working with the police, and their first assumption was that I was going to be setting people up to fall. I was an informant; either way I was snitching. Seeing me dressed in my work attire intimidated people, yet they'd still stop out of fear and ask me how I was doing.

I saw fear from both parties, Scotland Yard and the Streets. I was now looking after people on the witness protection project and the closer I made it to the top the more people reminded me that I was being watched and my past hadn't been forgotten. I knew the streets would always be watching me, some hoping I'd make it and others waiting for me to fall. I worked hard with Scotland Yard. I knew I needed to earn my stripes with them and I was. My work effort had its advantages and I out shined the other employees without a doubt. *I* was keeping the clients out of Southwark and in return the murders in our community were down and at risk youths were being managed.

I never forgot a client and once put into my care I guided them efficiently by the book. Hoping that they, like me, would take full advantage of the support and opportunities the project offered. Not once after joining the Makeda Weaver project did I think about returning to the streets.

"Did you hear, Que? I got a job," my client sounded over the moon on the other end of the phone.

"Yeah, I heard," I said, proud that he had made it on my

watch. I was the first mentor on the Witness Protection Project to say that my client had found employment and settled into society without re-offending. He now works as a journalist for a magazine company in Brixton called *Live Magazine*. They help kids leave the streets by finding individuals careers in areas where they show an interest.

"Everybody's good at something, you know!" my client explained to me when he went through the job description of his new role in the work force and he was right. I'd learnt years ago that I had the ability to captivate an audience and hold their attention. But I never in my wildest dreams believed that the same people who detained me would be the same people respecting my ability to reach those on the edge.

CHAPTER: TWENTY-FIVE |

Now, as I sit in a class with thirty four other students all from different walks of life I feel just inches away from success. Not only am I studying Law but I have graduated in Counselling.

I remember the first time I stepped foot in Birkbeck University, walking through the gates and coming face to face with the large glass building was intermediating. All the strange intelligent people rushing around excited me. I had finally made it to University. A part of me wanted to turn around and leave but I didn't. I couldn't. I thought about all the people who I lost, my mum, Poops, Lamont. I had to make positive the anxiety I was feeling. I wasn't just changing for me but also for them, I was scared before. Wanting to succeed with my ambitions and dreams but afraid I'd never make it.

Not knowing what to expect as I stood outside of my class peering in at all the adult students I made a choice that this is where my new life would begin. I took a seat and listened to the lecturer speak and was amazed that what she was saying made sense. I looked around me and saw faces of all races and people of all kinds of walks of life; I wondered *was I the youngest in the class?* I really couldn't tell but after listening to the other students answer and ask questions I was pretty sure I was the only person in the room who had been on the other side of the law.

"What would you do if you encountered a dead person on

the street after having been run by a car ahead?" The female lecturer asked a group of students who were deep in debate before the lesson came to an end. One at a time they all stood up and described how they would react to such a distressing situation. I thought about that question a lot while the other students elaborated. Having been on the other side gave me an advantage; something I knew would help me dramatically in my chosen subject. I was no longer naive to the right and wrongs of the law; I'd prepared myself for this transition and had educated myself every chance I got. Makeda Weaver gave me the opportunity to explore another side of my community. The side that needed help.

"Excuse me!" I called out to the lecturer when the lesson was over and the last of the students were leaving. I was unsure how to approach her.

"Can I ask you something?" I asked when I had caught her attention.

"Yes of course." She politely answered and proceeded to sit back at her desk. The lecturer and I spoke briefly of the requirements of the course; it was amazing that we could have such a relaxed conversation.

"Could a person who has spent time in prison as an inmate ever becomes a lawyer? Is it possible?"

"No." she replied immediately shattering my dreams. Once again my criminal past had come back to haunt. I thought; *will I never be free of my one crime.*

Reality had knocked me but I wasn't down. I don't consider myself to be rich, or even wealthy. I still struggle financially as the working class do but I am proud to struggle as a working class man. Gone are the days were I'd break into a strangers home or an establishment for petty cash or a plasma TV. When things get tough I now turn to my support mechanism my time in prison living off change taught me to work hard for the things I obtain. Not just material things but fundamental things too. I could have easily gone back to my reckless old life style, but. *What would have*

184

been the point? When I wake up in the morning and look in the mirror I want to be the person I see staring back at me. Gwenton Sloley. Calm, successful, capable Gwenton Sloley. Not the guy that people are threatened by because of his violent reputation and robbery conviction.

Most people coming from where I've been see pain, when they look in the mirror; frustration and guilt are also amongst the things they see when their reflection blinks back, I know because I see it too. Guilt from the pain I've caused other families to suffer and the guilt I feel when I see the families of my deceased friends. Because although individuals I helped them along their path to destruction just as much as others helped me. Every human wants to belong to something. If not they exclude themselves. Society can appreciate that 'status, symbols, territory and turf' are immensely important to many young people. It often makes me wonder: had I and others like me applied ourselves to our education and career choices the way we had our street life would half of the deceased in our generation still have their lives.

Now when I look in the mirror I'm proud at the individual man that looks back at me, he is not just any random man, he's me. No longer afraid of my feelings I'm in control. Instead of pretending to be a 'bad man' I have chosen to be a business man. I make it my business to be aware of my actions in my community. I have worked with Islington Council, Lewisham Council, Hackney Council and Hackney and Islington College's. All projects and charities that have been set up to help people who have fallen in with the wrong crowd. It seems daunting to me that teenagers' dying at the hands of people wielding guns and knives doesn't register in the minds of most people, they only register fear and most people don't even care until they have lost one of their own.

Currently I'm employed for Makeda Weaver Project, an outreach project run out of Shian housing association. I mentor young men who have been in similar situations I'd faced growing up, giving them advice and guidance or sometimes just a listening ear. It's easy for me to hear their stories and feel their struggles because I can connect with them. I have actually lived their fear and still live it as I slowly transform into gentleman.

Working with ex offenders I have found that the majority of them have learning difficulties or mental difficulties that haven't yet been dealt with. I will say that as a society parents, teachers and police need to work closer together. I have watched children being thrown out of classrooms for being disruptive a thousand times throughout my years in school, yet no one has bothered to find out why. People are often reluctant to express their feelings willingly but a little support could mean all the difference. It's difficult and sometimes hypocritical to say that young people offend because their communities lack resources. I grew up in Hackney, a borough that has a total of 62 parks, gardens and open spaces totalling about 330 hectares, ranging from the largest concentration of football pitches at Hackney Marshes to the historic settings of Springfield and Clissold parks. Boredom is not an excuse for crime yet many of the youth blame their antics on not having anything to do.

Throughout my childhood I searched for someone to teach me, lead me down the right road and inspire me to live for more than money, chasing hood dreams and committing crimes. I traveled from Jamaica and resided on Stoke Newington estate where I gain respect from the local rude boys selling drugs and creating wars between post codes for nothing but respect and wealth. Nobody told me that there were people in my community that wanted to help me. People who dedicated their lives to stopping gangs and find positive places for the youth in today's society.

I left my estate many times whilst searching for guidance during hard times. Little did I know but one of my biggest inspirations would come from the very place I was escaping. Leroy Logan was as far as I could tell the most powerful and influential police officer I'd met. When I met Leroy he was working at Stoke Newington police station as Superintendent of Hackney. We clicked instantly; he was all about helping the youths and so down to earth. So much so that at times I forgot he was a police officer.

Leroy would always find time to have a meet with me to see I was still on the right track; he even put me forward for a job working with Hackney YOS (Youth Offending Service) alongside their gang team. Everything was in place he'd even go as far as to make plans to take me to the Beijing Olympics. That was before he was assigned to the post of head of the 2012 Olympics. It was a great offer for him and he expressed to me that with all the hard work he'd put it when it became his time for retirement he could retire on a healthy pension. Leroy also expressed his discretion towards the post if anything went wrong he would be the first to blame. I knew like me Leroy wouldn't let fear get in the way of his accomplishments.

CHAPTER: TWENTY-SIX |

Unfortunately, my time spent with Leroy was short lived. We knew our time of hanging out was close coming to an end, I would never forget the words he spoke to me before we departed into our own destinies. It was at the Mothers against Guns movie premier in west-end that I and Leroy last hung out, after the show we went for soft drink and he sat me down and explained that I had a long and hard road ahead of me.

"Make sure you stay positive Que and if you ever feel like your slipping back into the street don't hesitate to give me a call"

I didn't quite understand what Leroy meant at the time but the one thing I knew was that If I was going to make it I had to it stick at my gang re-habilitation work .

Two years later I was sitting in the City Hall having a gangs meeting with the Mayor of London who was Boris Johnson at the time along with *Paul Casman, Richard Taylor (Damilola Taylor father), professor Goss, Boris Johnson and Deputy Mare Kit Môn house.*

I was taken aback by the BBC camera crew, then I looked over at the far end of the table and saw Viv Ahmum (*Chair, The Federation of Black and Asian Drugs Workers and Chief Officer, In-evolve.*) on the far end of the large round table we were seated around. I had never met Viv before this meeting but as we caught each other's eye he nodded my way and I nodded back. To me it was a mark of respect as if to say; Yes *brother were here.* We didn't have to speak the energy spoke through our eyes and at that moment I saw all of what Leroy was teaching me. I remember feeling like I was at a meeting with my uncle Less talking business with some of his rich friends. The way Viv Ahmum spoke to the room of twenty some people including the Mayor was like a pastor speaking to his church. He had my heart racing, speaking with a powerful clear voice he demanded attention but still remained very in tune with his community.

I went home that night thinking I too want to become a motivational speaker and would spend the next two years practicing my public speaking. It wasn't long before I started to master the art of taking control and captivating the attention of groups big enough to fill the Arsenal Stadium. It was there that I grabbed at the Attention of Council officers, Trident officers, the Makeda Weaver family and the Little Makeda Weaver. I also got the privileged to speak in front of my teacher Leroy as he was in attendance constantly supporting my struggle.

Leroy Logan spoke shortly after me; his wide smile expressed how proud he was to see that his work hadn't fallen on deaf ears. He started of his speech by saying "I class Gwenton as a good *friend* of mine." I could see the look on the faces of the people in the crowd. They were in shock whilst Leroy continued to commend me for my hard work and effort.

Today I am still a mentor on the Makeda Weaver project working closely with the YOS and the Lewisham police and its probation service in a lower end wittiness protection project called Trilogy Plus. We work with all the young children/adults that other associations turn away. Most people don't know of the new laws the police have implemented to deal with gang members, our support groups educate them on what is considered gang activity. For example; Joint Enterprise - If three or more people are present when a crime is committed, no matter how small or big apart you played you will all get charged with the same offence.

Amongst my other colleagues I work alongside two mentors,

two police officers and two resettlement officers. We work as a close team and have been very successful in rehabilitating ex-offenders and stopping the young offending. This is the first time I have ever worked closely with a policeman; I respected them as individuals instead of an enemy in a uniform. Police officers all over London are trying to engage with young people but it is not them who is failing it the youths. So much talk about 'being real' and 'being loyal' when the people who have earned respect are disregarded as 'pigs.' When I look at the youths of today hanging around in gangs and committing useless crimes I feel ashamed, ashamed that I shared their history. I'm kept busy most days, with work. I hardly associate with old friends and nightclubs are a thing of the past. On the weekends and evenings I take a small group of young men to the gym, being the responsible adult and listening to their expatiations of life reminds me of how blind I was between the ages of 15-19. I am admired by those young people, I don't influence them but I give them advice and guidance. I hear them speaking about their good friends and their boys and remind them that while there out on the street they are alone. Your family is the only people who will love or even care enough to folk out in your favour to bury you. I know firsthand that coming from a broken and abusive home can hinder a child's sprit and force them to seek compassion or ever respect from a different source. I have given my testimony now over a hundred times, be it in front of a crowded hall or to a single person and it wasn't until I started being honest with myself that people started to open up and be honest too.

Looking back on the life I once lead, I never once would have thought that I'd be working alongside police officers, helping them and being respected and invited to meetings with people such as Viv Ahmum and the mayor. I'm proud of my accomplishments but I don't want to be alone as I stand the only true survivor reformed from the streets to Scotland Yard.